GNU Anubis Reference Manual

A catalogue record for this book is available from the Hong Kong Public Libraries.

Published in Hong Kong by Samurai Media Limited.

Email: info@samuraimedia.org

ISBN 978-988-8381-53-1

Short Contents

Table of Contents

1 Overview

GNU Anubis is an SMTP message submission daemon. Its purpose is to receive outgoing messages, optionally perform some manipulations over their content, and to forward altered messages to the mail transport agent.

A usual mail sending scheme looks as follows: the user composes his message using *mail user agent* (*MUA* for short). Once the message is composed, the user sends it. While sending, the MUA connects to the *mail transport agent* (*MTA* for short) and passes it the message for delivery. The figure below illustrates this interaction:

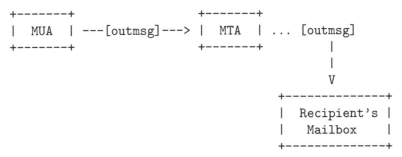

As shown in this figure, outgoing message (*outmsg*) reaches the recipient's mailbox unaltered.

However, there are situations where it may be necessary to modify the outgoing message before it reaches MTA. For example, the user might wish to sign outgoing messages with his PGP key, because his MUA does not support this operation.

In such cases, installing GNU Anubis between the MUA and MTA allows the user to perform additional processing on the sent message. The figure below illustrates this concept:

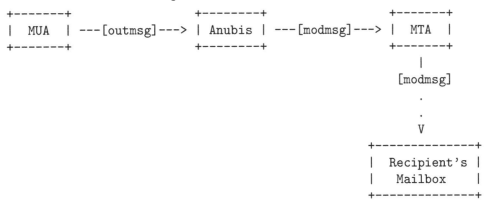

The outgoing message is modified by GNU Anubis, and it is the resulting message (*modmsg*) that reaches the MTA.

GNU Anubis is able to perform a wide set of operations on messages, such as modifying headers or body, encrypting or signing messages with GPG (GNU Privacy Guard) keys, installing secure tunnels to MTA using TLS/SSL encryption, tunneling messages through SOCKS proxies, etc.

When the set of built-in operations is not enough, administrators can
define new ones using Guile, a *GNU's Ubiquitous Intelligent Language for
Extensions*.

Apart from configurable operations, GNU Anubis always performs *SMTP
session normalization*, a process that ensures that the SMTP stream coming
out of Anubis complies with the RFC 2821, even if the incoming stream does
not. In particular, Anubis removes any extra whitespace appearing between
'`MAIL FROM:`' or '`SMTP TO`' command and its argument.

Message processing is controlled by two configuration files: a system-wide
one that affects functionality of the system as a whole, and user configuration
files, which modify Anubis behaviour on a per-user basis.

2 Glossary of Frequently Used Terms

Authentication
> A process whereby Anubis determines authenticity of the connecting party, its user name and configuration settings.

Protocol
> A standard for information exchange. Protocol defines specific wording and control flow for communications between two or more programs, devices or systems.

SMTP
> Simple Mail Transport Protocol is a common mechanism for exchanging mail across a network. This was described initially in RFC 821, and subsequently extended by more documents, the most recent one being RFC 5321.

Daemon
> A process that runs in the background, doing automated processing.

Server
> A server provides information or other services for its clients. Most network protocols are client–server based. This term often refers to hardware, but it can also refer (and we're using it that way) to a particular program or process, on that machine, which provides the service.

Proxy
> A program, which goes between MUA and MTA. It can be used as a gateway to the outside world, while using a firewall. In this case a host under the firewall sends data to the proxy server, which in turn forwards it to a server outside, receives its replies, and passes them back to the internal host.

Guile
> GNU's Ubiquitous Intelligent Language for Extensions. It provides a Scheme interpreter conforming to the R5RS language specification. GNU Anubis uses Guile as its extension language. For more information about Guile, Section "Overview" in *The Guile Reference Manual*.

GPG
> GNU Privacy Guard, a tool compatible with *PGP* (*Pretty Good Privacy*).

3 Authentication

When GNU Anubis accepts incoming connection, it first has to identify the remote party, i.e. to determine whether it is authorised to use Anubis resources and, if so, what configuration settings to use during the session. We call this process *authentication*. The exact method of authentication depends on Anubis *operation mode*. Currently there are three modes:

proxy   No authentication is performed. Anubis switches to the unprivileged user (see Section 4.2.6 [user-unprivileged], page 23) and acts as an *SMTP proxy*.

transparent
               Anubis relies on AUTH service (`identd`) to authenticate users. This is the default mode. It is compatible with versions of GNU Anubis up to 3.6.2.

auth   This mode uses SMTP AUTH mechanism to authenticate incoming connections. See Appendix A [Pixie-Dixie], page 59, original description of this mode.

Both modes have their advantages and deficiencies, which you need to weigh carefully before choosing which one to use. They are discussed below:

Transparent ('traditional') mode.

Deficiencies:

1. The user must have `identd` installed on his machine.
2. The user must have a system account on the machine running GNU Anubis (though the system administrator may relax this limitation by using user name translation, see Section 4.3 [TRANSLATION Section], page 24).

Advantages:

1. Relative simplicity. No user database is necessary.
2. Authentication is performed immediately after connecting.

Auth mode.

Deficiencies:

1. A user database is needed
2. MUAs of the users must be able to perform ESMTP AUTH.[1]

Advantages:

1. Improved reliability.

---

[1] It is not a serious restriction, however. Users may install Anubis on their machines for the sole purpose of SMTP authentication, as Pixie-Dixie suggests.

2. Users do not have to run `identd` on their machines.

3. Users are not required to have accounts on the machine where Anubis runs.

4. Users can remotely modify their configuration files.

3.1 User Database

A *User Database* is a storage system where GNU Anubis keeps *user credentials*, i.e. data necessary for authenticating and authorizing users. The exact way of storing these data is described further in this manual. In this section we treat user database as an abstraction layer.

The user database consists of *records*. Each record keeps information about a particular *user*. A record consists of four *fields*. A field may contain some value, or be empty, in which case we say that it has *null* value.

The fields are:

SMTP AUTHID
>   SMTP authentication ID of the user.

AUTH PASSWORD
>   SMTP password.

ACCOUNT   System user name.

CONFIG   Path to the configuration file.

The first two fields are mandatory and must always have non-null values. No two records in the database may have the same value of `SMTP AUTHID` field. When `anubis` is trying to authenticate a user, it first looks up in the database a record with the value of `SMTP AUTHID` field matching AUTHID given by the user. If no such entry is found, authentication fails. Otherwise, `anubis` goes on and compares the password supplied by the user with that from `AUTH PASSWORD` field. If they match, authentication succeeds and `anubis` passes to authorization state.

In this state, it first determines the user ID (UID) to switch to. If the `ACCOUNT` field is not null, its value is used as account login name. If it is null, `anubis` uses the privileges of the *default not privileged user*, specified by `user-notprivileged` statement in the global configuration file (see Section 4.2.6 [Security Settings], page 23).

The final step is to parse the *user configuration file*. If `CONFIG` field is not null, its value is used as absolute path to the configuration file. Otherwise, `anubis` searches for file `~/.anubisrc` (where '~' denotes home directory for the system account obtained on the previous step) and if such a file exists, loads it.

3.2 Database URL

Anubis database is identified by its *URL*, or *Universal Resource Locator*. A `URL` consists of following elements (square brackets enclose optional elements):

    proto://[[user[:password]@]host]/path[params]

where:

proto   Specifies the database *protocol*. The protocol describes how the database is to be accessed. In a way, it may be regarded as specifying the database *type*. Currently, GNU Anubis supports the following database protocols:

'text'	A plain text file with users' credentials.
'gdbm'	GDBM database
'mysql'	MySQL database
'pgsql'	PostgreSQL database
'postgres'	Alias for 'pgsql'.

These protocols are described in detail below.

user   The name of the user authorized to access the database.

password   Password for the above user.

host   Domain name or IP address of a machine running the database.

path   A *path* to the database. The exact meaning of this element depends on the database protocol. It is described in detail when discussing particular protocols.

params   A list of protocol-dependent parameters. Each parameter consists of the *parameter name*, or *keyword* and its *value* separated by a equals sign:

              keyword=name

These protocols are described in detail below.

Multiple parameters are separated by semicolons.

3.2.1 Plain text databases

A simplest database is a plain text file, with lines representing *records*. Empty lines and lines beginning with '#' (*comments*) sign are ignored. A record consists of *fields*, separated by colons (':', ASCII 58). If ':' character occurs as a part of a field, it must be escaped by a single backslash character ('\\', ASCII 92). Each record must contain at least two and no more than four fields:

1. SMTP 'AUTHID'.

2. SMTP password.

3. Account name.

4. Pathname of the user configuration file.

URL syntax

The URL syntax for this type of databases is quite simple:

```
text:path
```

where *path* specifies absolute file name of the database file.

3.2.2 Databases in GDBM format

The protocol value 'gdbm' specifies a *GDBM database*. For the detailed description of GDBM system Section "Introduction" in *The GNU DBM Manual*.

Technically speaking, each GDBM record consists of a *key* and *content*. Its key holds the value of SMTP 'AUTHID', whereas its content holds SMTP password, system account name and path to user configuration file, separated by commas. As it was with 'text' databases, the two last fields are optional.

The URL syntax for GDBM databases is:

```
gdbm:path
```

where *path* specifies absolute file name of the database file.

3.2.3 MySQL and PostgreSQL

This is the most flexible database format. GNU Anubis 4.2 supports MySQL[2] and PostgreSQL[3] interfaces. No matter which of them you use, the implementation details are hidden behind a single consistent Anubis interface.

GNU Anubis supposes that all user data are kept in a single database table. This table must have at least four columns for storing SMTP 'AUTHID', SMTP password, system account name and path to user configuration file. Among those, only the last two may have NULL values. There is no restriction on the name of the database or the authentication table, nor on its column names. This information may be specified in URL as discussed below.

URL syntax

```
proto://[[user[:password]@]host/]dbname[params]
```

Proto describes the database type to use. Use 'mysql' for MySQL databases and 'pgsql' or 'postgres' for PostgreSQL databases.

Optional *user* and *password* specify authentication credentials for accessing the database.

Host sets the domain name or IP address of the machine running the database. It may be omitted if the database resides on 'localhost'.

The database name is specified by the *dbname* element.

---

[2] See http://www.mysql.com.
[3] See http://www.postgres.org.

Further details needed for connecting to the database are given by URL parameters. All of them have reasonable default values, so you'll have to specify only those parameters that differ from the default. The following parameters are defined:

port=*number*

> Specifies port number the database server is listening on. If it is not given, the behavior depends on the value of the `socket` parameter (see below). If `socket` is not present, the program will use the default port number for the given protocol (i.e. 3306 for 'mysql' and 5432 for 'pgsql'.

socket=*string*

> Specifies the UNIX file name of the socket to connect to. This parameter cannot be used together with `port` (see above).

bufsize=*number*

> Sets length of the buffer for storing SQL queries. Default is 1024 bytes.

table=*string*

> Specifies name of the database table with the authentication data. Default is 'users'.

authid=*string*

> Specifies the name of a column in `table` which holds 'AUTHID' value. Default is 'authid'.

passwd=*string*

> Specifies the name of a column in `table` which holds the user password. Default is 'passwd'.

account=*string*

> Specifies the name of a column in `table` which holds the name of system account to be used for this 'AUTHID'. Default is 'account'.

rcfile=*string*

> Specifies the name of a column in `table` which holds the path to the user's configuration file. Default is 'rcfile'.

When using a MySQL database ('mysql://'), database parameters and access credentials are first read from the file /etc/my.cnf, if it exists. This file called *option file* in 'MySQL' parlance (see Section "option-files" in *MySQL Manual*) is organized in groups, each group beginning with the group name in square brackets on a separate line. Within a group, each non-empty line consists of a MySQL option name, optionally followed by an equals sign and the value. By default, the values from the 'anubis' group are read.

Two additional parameters are provided to fine-tune this behavior:

```
options-file=file
```
> Read options from *file* instead of **/etc/my.cnf**. An empty value
> ('**options-file=**'), disables using the options file.

```
options-group=name
```
> Set the name of the group in the MySQL configuration file, from
> which to read configuration options.

3.3 Managing the Database

Managing the user database is a complex task, which looks differently from
administrator's and user's point of view. Administrators have all privileges
on the database, they can add new records and delete or modify existing
ones. Users, of course, do not have such ample rights. The only thing a user
is able to do is to maintain his own record in the database, provided that he
already has one.

3.3.1 Administrators

All administrative tasks are done via the **anubisadm** command — a multi-
purpose tool for Anubis administrators.

The command usage syntax is:

```
anubisadm command [options] database-url
```

where *command* specifies the operation to be performed on the database, *options* give additional operation-specific parameters, and *database-url* specifies the database to operate upon.

All administrative tasks can be subdivided into the following five cate-
gories:

- Creating the Database
- Listing Database Records
- Adding New Records
- Removing Existing Records
- Modifying Existing Records

3.3.1.1 Creating the Database

To create a database, use **anubisadm --create** (or **anubisadm -c**).
Anubisadm will read database entries from the standard input and write
them to the database. The standard input is supposed to be formatted as a
text database (see Section 3.2.1 [text], page 7).

For example, to create a GDBM database from plain text file **userlist**,
use the following command

```
anubisadm --create gdbm:/etc/anubis.db < userlist
```

Similarly, to create an initially empty database, type

```
anubisadm --create gdbm:/etc/anubis.db < /dev/null
```

Notice, that if you use SQL database format, `--create` command does not imply creating the database structure! So, before running

```
anubisadm --create mysql://localhost/dbname < userlist
```

make sure you create the underlying database structure (including granting privileges to the `anubis` user), via the usual procedure. Please refer to corresponding database manual for the detailed instructions on this.

It is sometimes necessary to convert an existing user database from one format (protocol) to another. For example, suppose you have been running GDBM database (`text:/etc/anubis.db`) for some time, but now it has grown so big that you decided to switch to PostgreSQL database to improve performance. To do so, first create the database using postgres utilities. Then run

```
anubisadm --list text:/etc/anubis.db | \
   anubisadm --create pgsql://localhost/dbname
```

That's all there is to it!

3.3.1.2 Listing Database Records

The `--list` (or `-l`) option lists the existing database:

```
anubisadm --list gdbm:/etc/anubis.db
```

By default it displays all records from the database.

Among its other uses, such invocation is handy for converting user database to another format (see Section 3.3.1.1 [Create], page 10).

If you wish to list only a particular record, specify the AUTHID using `--authid` (`-i`) option. For example, to list the record for AUTHID 'test', type:

```
example$ anubisadm --list --authid test gdbm:/etc/anubis.db
```

3.3.1.3 Adding New Records

To add a new record use the `--add` (`-a`) option. Additional data are specified via the following options:

`-i string`
`--authid=string`
> Specify the user SMTP AUTHID.

`-p string`
`--password=string`
> Specify the user password.

`-u string`
`--user=string`
> Specify the system user name for this AUTHID.

`-f string`
`--rcfile=string`
> Specify configuration file to be used for this user.

For example, the following command adds a record with `SMTP AUTHID` 'test', password 'guessme' and maps it to the system account 'gray':

```
anubisadm --add --authid test --password guessme \
          --user gray gdbm:/etc/anubis.db
```

3.3.1.4 Removing Existing Records

Removing a record is quite straightforward: use the `--remove` (`-r`) option and supply the `AUTHID` to delete via the `--authid` option. For example, to remove the record created in the previous subsection, run:

```
anubisadm --remove --authid test gdbm:/etc/anubis.db
```

3.3.1.5 Modifying Existing Records

To modify an existing record use the `--modify` (`-m`) option. The record is identified via the `--authid` option. The following options supply the changed values:

`-p string`
`--password=string`
>   Specify new user password.

`-u string`
`--user=string`
>   Specify new system user name for this `AUTHID`.

`-f string`
`--rcfile=string`
>   Specify the user's configuration file.

For example, the following command changes the name of configuration file for the user 'smith':

```
anubisadm --authid smith \
          --rcfile=/var/spool/anubis/common gdbm:/etc/anubis.db
```

3.3.1.6 Summary of All Administrative Commands

- Usage

  ```
  anubisadm command [options] database-url
  ```

- Commands:

  `-c`
  `--create`   Create the database.

  `-l`
  `--list`   List the contents of an existing database.

  `-a`
  `--add`   Add a new record.

  `-m`
  `--modify`   Modify an existing record.

```
-r
```
`--remove`   Remove an existing record.

`--version`
             Display program version number and exit.

`--help`   Display short usage summary and exit.

- Options:

`-i string`
`--authid=string`
             Specify the authid to operate upon. This option is manda-
             tory for `--add`, `--modify` and `--remove` commands. It may
             also be used with `--list` command.

`-p string`
`--password=string`
             Specify the password for the authid. This option is manda-
             tory for `--add`, `--modify` and `--remove` commands.

`-u string`
`--user=string`
             Specify the system user name corresponding to the given au-
             thid. It may be used with `--add`, `--modify`, and `--remove`
             commands.

`-f string`
`--rcfile=string`
             Specify the rc file to be used for this authid. The option may
             be used with `--add`, `--modify`, and `--remove` commands.

3.3.2 Users

Users maintain their database records via the **anubisusr** command. We
suggest invoking **anubisusr** from your `~/.profile`, which will make sure
that your configuration file is up to date when you log in.[4]

Usage

    anubisusr [options] [smtp-url]

where *smtp-url* is a URL of your GNU Anubis server. Notice that if it lacks
user name and password, then **anubisusr** will first try to retrieve them from
your `~/.netrc` file (see Section "netrc" in *netrc manual page*), and if not
found, it will prompt you to supply them.

---

[4] Make sure to run **anubisusr** in background, so it does not slow down your normal
login sequence.

Options

`-m` *mech*
`--mechanism` *mech*

> Use the SASL mechanism *mech*. Give this option several times to set a list of allowed mechanisms.

`--file=`*file*
`-f` *file*   Sets the user configuration file name (default is `.anubisrc`).

`--netrc+`*file*
`-n` *file*   Sets the name of the automatic login configuration file (default is `.netrc`).

`-v`
`--verbose`

> Verbose output. Multiple options increase verbosity. Maximum verbosity level is 3.

Options controlling encryption:

`--disable-tls`
`-d`   Disable the use of TLS encryption.

`--tls-cafile=`*file*
`-C` *file*   Sets the name of certificate authority file to use when verifying the server certificate.

`--tls-priorities=`*list*

> Sets cipher suite preferences to use. The *list* argument may contain a single initial keyword or be a colon-separated list of TLS keywords. The description of TLS keywords is well beyond the scope of this document. Please refer to Section "Priority Strings" in *GnuTLS Manual*, for a detailed discussion.
>
> Default priority list is 'NORMAL'.

Informational options:

`--version`

> Display program version number and exit.

`--help`   Display short usage summary and exit.

4 Configuration

The behavior of GNU Anubis is controlled by two configuration files. The *system configuration file*, `/etc/anubisrc`, supplies system-wide settings that affect all users. This file is usually owned by root. The *user configuration file* specifies what GNU Anubis should do for a particular user. By default it is located in `~/.anubisrc`. This location can be changed if `anubis` operates in auth mode. The permissions of a user configuration file must be set to 0600 (u=rw,g=,o=), otherwise GNU Anubis won't accept the file.

Lexical Structure

Both configuration files use simple line-oriented syntax. Each line introduces a single statement. A statement consists of *words*, each word being defined as a contiguous sequence of non-whitespace symbols. The word may be composed of alphanumeric characters and any of the following punctuation symbols: '_', '.', '/', '-'. Any arbitrary sequence of characters enclosed in a pair of double quotes is also recognized as a word. Such a sequence is called *quoted string*.

Quoted strings follow the same syntax rules as in the C language. A backslash character '\' alters the meaning of the character following it. This special construct is called *escape sequence*. When processing an escape sequence, Anubis removes it from the string and replaces it with a single character as described in the following table:

Sequence	Replaced with
\a	Audible bell character (ASCII 7)
\b	Backspace character (ASCII 8)
\e	Escape (ASCII (ASCII 27)
\f	Form-feed character (ASCII 12)
\n	Newline character (ASCII 10)
\r	Carriage return character (ASCII 13)
\t	Horizontal tabulation character (ASCII 9)
\v	Vertical tabulation character (ASCII 11)

Table 4.1: Backslash escapes

A backslash followed by any character not listed above is replaced by the character alone. This can be used, in particular, for inserting '"' character within a string, as in the example below:

```
"This string contains \"quoted string\"."
```

Similarly, a backslash followed by a newline is replaced by the newline itself. Thus, the following two strings are equivalent:

```
"This string is split\nover two lines"
```

```
"This string is split\
over two lines"
```

The familiar shell *here document* syntax can be used to produce a word containing several lines of text. The syntax is:

```
<<[-]delimiter
    text
delimiter
```

If "here document" starts with '<<-', then all leading tab characters are stripped from input lines and the line containing *delimiter*. This allows to indent here-document in a natural fashion.

To summarize all the above, let's consider an example:

```
first-word "second word" <<-EOT
                          Third word
                          containing several
                          lines of text
                          EOT
```

This line contains three words: 'first-word', 'second word' and the third one composed of the three lines between the 'EOT' markers.

If a statement is very long, it may be split among several lines of text. To do so, end each line with a backslash ('\'), immediately before the newline, as in:

```
a very long statement\
  occupying several lines\
  of text
```

A '#' in a line starts a *comment*. The '#' character and the rest of the line following it are ignored. Comments may appear anywhere in the configuration file, except within a command line or a "here-document" construct. A line containing just a comment (with optional whitespace before it) is effectively blank, and is ignored. For example:

```
# This is a comment
if header[Subject] :re "No.*"  # This is also a comment
  guile-process action-name This # is not a comment!!!
fi
```

Logical Structure

Statements in a configuration file are grouped into *sections*. Each section has its name. A section begins with one of the following constructs:

```
BEGIN name
---BEGIN name---
```

and ends with one of the following constructs:

```
END
---END---
```

Notice, that both 'BEGIN' and 'END' must be uppercase. When using the second form, any amount of whitespace is allowed between the three dashes and the word.

Sections cannot be nested.

There are five predefined sections, whose names are in uppercase. The user may define his own sections, which may then be referred to from the RULE section as subroutines (see Section 5.6.2 [Call Action], page 33).

The predefined section names are:

AUTH   Defines authentication mechanisms.

CONTROL
              This section specifies the basic GNU Anubis behavior. Its presence is required in the system configuration file. It may be used in the user configuration file to override the system-wide settings.

TRANSLATION
              This section specifies a translation map for mapping remote user names to local ones. It may be used only in the system-wide configuration file.

GUILE   Configures the Guile interpreter. This section is allowed in both configuration files.

RULE   Defines rules that for altering the message contents.

4.1 AUTH Section

The AUTH session controls various aspects of authentication mode.

smtp-greeting-message *text*   [Option]
    Configures the greeting message issued by GNU Anubis upon accepting SMTP connection.

smtp-help-message *help-text*   [Option]
    Defines the message issued in response to SMTP HELP command. *Help-text* is a list of strings. Each string from the list will be displayed on a separate response line.

sasl-password-db *url*   [Option]
    Sets URL of the user database (see Section 3.1 [User Database], page 6).

sasl-allowed-mech *mech-list*   [Option]
    Defines the list of allowed authentication methods.

sasl-service *name*   [Option]
    Sets the SASL *service name*. It is used, among others, with GSSAPI authentication method. Default is 'anubis'.

sasl-hostname *name*   [Option]
    Sets the SASL hostname. By default, the server determines it automatically. If it happens to make a wrong guess, you can fix it using this directive.

`sasl-realm` *name*   [Option]
> Sets the SASL realm. By default, the local domain is used as SASL realm
> (see Section 4.2.1 [Basic Settings], page 18).

4.2 CONTROL Section

The 'CONTROL' section defines basic GNU Anubis behavior. If used in the
system-wide configuration file, it applies to all users in the system. Each
user can have a 'CONTROL' section in his configuration file, to customize his
personal settings. Of course, not all options can be set or changed by the
user. Some options can only be set in the system configuration file, and
some only in the user configuration file. By default, options specified in the
user configuration file have a **higher** priority than those specified in system
configuration file.

All option names are case insensitive, so that `bind` or `BIND` or `BiNd` all
refer to the same option.

4.2.1 Basic Settings

> (*The information in this node may be obsolete or otherwise inac-
> curate.* This message will disappear, once this node revised.)

`bind` [*host:*]*port*   [Option]
> Specify the TCP port on which GNU Anubis listens for connections. The
> default *host* value is 'INADDR_ANY', which means that anyone can connect
> to GNU Anubis. The default *port* number is 24 (private mail system).
> This option is available only in the system configuration file.
>
> For example, to bind GNU Anubis to port 25 (SMTP) and limit its clients
> only to those from 'localhost', set the following in your system config-
> uration file:
>
> ```
> bind localhost:25
> ```

`remote-mta` *host*[*:port*]   [Option]
> Specify a host name or IP address of the remote SMTP. GNU Anubis will
> forward mails to that server. The default *port* number is 25. This option
> is available in both configuration files.

`local-mta` *file-name* [*args*]   [Option]
> Execute a local SMTP server, which works on standard input and output
> (inetd-type program). For example:
>
> ```
> local-mta /usr/sbin/sendmail -bs
> ```
>
> The 'CONTROL' section must contain either `local-mta` or `remote-mta`, but
> not both.

`mode` *mode-name*   [Option]
> Selects Anubis operation mode. Allowed values for *mode-name* are:
>
> proxy

transparent
auth

See Chapter 3 [Authentication], page 5, for the detailed discussion of GNU Anubis operation modes.

read-entire-body *yes-or-no*   [Option]
> Normally, when processing a multi-part message with external filter (see Section 5.6.9 [External Processor], page 37), Anubis feeds only the first part to the filter. The rest of the message is copied verbatim. To alter this behavior so that your external program sees the entire message body, set `read-entire-body yes` in your control section.

incoming-mail-rule *string*   [Option]
> Declares the name of command section for incoming mail. Default is 'INCOMING'. This option is available only for system configuration file. See Chapter 10 [MDA Mode], page 53, for detailed description of incoming mail processing.

outgoing-mail-rule *string*   [Option]
> Declares the name of command section for outgoing mail. Default is 'RULE'. This option is available only for system configuration file.

smtp-command-rule *string*   [Option]
> Declares the name of command section for rewriting SMTP commands. Default is 'SMTP'. This option is available only for system configuration file. See Section 5.6.6 [Modifying SMTP Commands], page 35.

log-tag *string*   [Option]
> Tag syslog messages with *string*. Default is 'anubis'.

log-facility *string*   [Option]
> Use syslog facility *string* for logging. Valid argument values are: 'user', 'daemon', 'auth', 'authpriv', 'mail', 'cron', 'local0' through 'local7' (all names case-insensitive, optionally prefixed by 'log_'), or a decimal facility number. Default is 'mail'.

local-domain *string*   [Option]
> Set local domain name. By default, the domain name is defined as the part of the local host name following the first dot.
>
> Local domain name is used as SASL realm, unless overridden by 'sasl-realm' statement (see Section 4.1 [AUTH Section], page 17).

4.2.2 Output Settings

termlevel *level*   [Option]
> Defines logging verbosity level. Allowed values are:
>
> normal   Only errors are logged. This is the default level.

verbose   Produce more diagnostic output.

debug   Produce debugging output.

silent   Do not log anything.

This command is allowed only in the system configuration file.

logfile *file-name*   [Option]

This command sets the name of additional log file. GNU Anubis logs there messages about user's SMTP session, as defined by the 'loglevel' statement (see below). For example:

```
logfile "anubis.log"
```

This will direct additional logging to the `~/anubis.log` file in the user's home directory.

loglevel *level*   [Option]

This option defines verbosity level for the additional log file. It may be used only in user configuration file. Allowed values for *level* are:

fails   Log only failure messages.

all   Log all relevant messages.

tracefile *yes-or-no*   [Option]
tracefile *file-name*   [Option]

This option instructs **anubis** to log the execution of tests and actions from the RULE sections. This is useful for debugging configuration files.

When this option is used in the system-wide configuration file, only boolean argument is allowed. Using 'tracefile yes' enables logging of actions and tests to the default syslog channel. Using 'tracefile no' disables it.

When used in the user configuration file, a filename is allowed as an argument to this option. This allows you to explicitly specify to which file the tracing output should go. Otherwise, using 'tracefile yes' enables logging to the same file as 'logfile' (if possible).

HANG *delay*   [Option]

Do not use this option, unless you are developing or debugging Anubis!

This option instructs each child process to hang for the given number of seconds. Before hanging, the process issues the following diagnostic message:

```
Child process suspended for delay seconds
```

This option is useful for Anubis developers who wish to attach to a child process with debugger. After attaching, set the variable **_anubis_hang** to zero to continue processing. You may wish to add the following statement to your **.gdbinit** file:

```
set variable _anubis_hang=0
```

4.2.3 SOCKS Proxy

`socks-proxy host[:port]`   [Option]
  Enables tunneling incoming connections through a SOCKS proxy server,
  specified as an argument *host*. The default value for *port* is 1080, which
  is a common port number for SOCKS proxies.

`socks-v4 yes-or-no`   [Option]
  Use SOCKS protocol version 4. By default it is turned off, and version 5
  of the SOCKS protocol is used.

`socks-auth username:password`   [Option]
  Sets user name and password for the SOCKS proxy server.

4.2.4 ESMTP Authentication Settings

The following options set authentication credentials for ESMTP authentication. They are useful, for example, if your MTA requires such an authentication, but your MUA does not support it.

You can also use these statements in a 'SMTP' section. See Section 5.6.6
[Modifying SMTP Commands], page 35, for a detailed description of this
feature.

`esmtp-allowed-mech mech-list`   [Option]
  Defines the list of allowed authentication mechanisms. *Mech-list* is a list
  of valid authentication mechanism names separated by whitespace.

  Anubis selects the authentication method using the following algorithm:
  MTA presents a list of authentication methods it supports. For each element in *mech-list*, Anubis tests whether it is available in the list presented
  by MTA. If found, this method is selected. For example, suppose that
  the MTA reports the following supported mechanisms:

        PLAIN LOGIN CRAM-MD5 ANONYMOUS

  and in your configuration file you have:

        esmtp-allowed-mech DIGEST-MD5 CRAM-MD5 LOGIN

  Then, Anubis will select 'CRAM-MD5'.

`esmtp-require-encryption mech-list`   [Option]
  Declares the list of mechanisms that can be used only over a TLS encrypted channel. By default Anubis uses

        esmtp-require-encryption LOGIN PLAIN

  This prevents sending user password over an unencrypted connection.

`esmtp-auth-delayed yes-or-no`   [Option]
  By default, ESMTP authentication is attempted as early as possible,
  normally while handling the client 'EHLO' command.

  When this statement is set to '**yes**', authentication is delayed until the
  client issued the '**MAIL**' command. This will allow **anubis** to select au-

thentication credentials depending on the sender email. For a detailed description of this feature, see Section 5.6.6 [Modifying SMTP Commands], page 35.

`esmtp-auth-id` *authentication-id*   [Option]
>   Sets authentication ID (user name).

`esmtp-authz-id` *authorization-id*   [Option]
>   Sets authorization ID (user name).

`esmtp-password` *password*   [Option]
>   Sets ESTMP AUTH password.

`esmtp-auth` *username:password*   [Option]
>   This is a shortcut to set both authentication and authorization IDs and the password. It is equivalent to
>
> ```
> esmtp-auth-id username
> esmtp-authz-id username
> esmtp-password password
> ```

The following options specify authentication credentials for GSSAPI, DIGEST-MD5 and KERBEROS_V5 authentication mechanisms:

`esmtp-service` *service-name*   [Option]
>   Sets the name of GSSAPI service.

`esmtp-hostname` *hostname*   [Option]
>   Sets hostname of the machine.

`esmtp-generic-service` *servise-name*   [Option]
>   Sets generic service name.

`esmtp-passcode` *passcode*   [Option]
>   Sets passcode.

`esmtp-realm` *realm-name*   [Option]
>   Sets GSSAPI realm.

The following option is useful with the 'ANONYMOUS' authentication mechanism:

`esmtp-anonymous-token` *token*   [Option]
>   Sets the token to be used with the 'ANONYMOUS' authentication mechanism

4.2.5 Encryption Settings

`ssl` *yes-or-no*   [Option]
>   Enable or disable the TLS/SSL encryption between the MUA and the MTA. The default is 'no', but using the TLS/SSL encryption is recommended. You should also set your private key and certificate using the 'ssl-key' and 'ssl-cert' keywords (defined below).
>   See Chapter 8 [TLS/SSL], page 49, for details.

ssl-oneway *yes-or-no*   [Option]

Enable the *ONEWAY* encryption. Set `ssl-oneway yes`, if you want to use the TLS/SSL, but your MUA doesn't support ESMTP TLS/SSL. Using this option does not require setting the 'ssl-key' and 'ssl-cert' options.

ssl-priorities *list*   [Option]

Sets cipher suite preferences to use. The *list* argument is either a single initial keyword or a colon-separated list of TLS keywords. The description of TLS keywords is well beyond the scope of this document. Please refer to Section "Priority Strings" in *GnuTLS Manual*, for a detailed discussion.

The default priority list is 'NORMAL'.

ssl-cert *file-name*   [Option]

Specify the certificate for the TLS/SSL encryption.

Default for *file-name* is `anubis.pem`.

ssl-key *file-name*   [Option]

Set the private key for the TLS/SSL encryption.

The default *file-name* is `anubis.pem`.

ssl-cafile *file-name*   [Option]

Specify CA certificate file (supported only by GnuTLS).

4.2.6 Security Settings

The following options control various security settings.

drop-unknown-user *yes-or-no*   [Option]

If this option is set to 'yes', `anubis` drops sessions which failed verification by the IDENT service.

This option is in effect only in '`transparent`' mode.

Default is 'no'.

user-notprivileged *username*   [Option]

Defines the *unprivileged* user, i.e. the user with whose privileges `anubis` runs most of the time. This option is available only in the system configuration file. For example:

```
user-notprivileged "anubis"
```

Caution: This user must exist in the system user database (`/etc/passwd`).

rule-priority *value*   [Option]

This statement defines the order of execution of the system and user **RULE** sections (See Chapter 5 [Rule System], page 27, for a detailed description). It is available only in system configuration file.

Allowed values are:

`system`   First execute the system section, then the user one.

user   First execute the user section, then the system one.

system-only
              Execute only the system `RULE` section.

user-only
              Execute only the user `RULE` section.

`control-priority` *value*   [Option]
    Sets the order of processing `CONTROL` sections. This option is available
    only in system configuration file.

    Allowed values are:

system   The system `CONTROL` section is processed first. Notice, that
              this means that the user may override the system settings in
              his configuration file. This is the default setting.

user   The user `CONTROL` section is processed first. Thus, the system-
              wide settings always override users' private settings.

4.3 TRANSLATION Section

The 'TRANSLATION' section specifies how to translate remote or local user
names, or host names or addresses, to local user names. The 'TRANSLATION'
section is available only in the system configuration file. The syntax is:

```
---BEGIN TRANSLATION---
translate  [user@]address into  username
...
---END---
```

address means host name or IP address. You can also specify '`0.0.0.0`',
and it means any address ('`INADDR_ANY`').

    For example:

```
BEGIN TRANSLATION
translate jack@example.net into john
END
```

This rule will allows the remote user '`jack`' at '`example.net`' to use the
configuration file of the local user '`john`'.

    In the contrast, this statement:

```
translate example.net into john
```

means that *all* users at '`example.net`' are allowed to use the local john's
configuration file.

4.4 GUILE Section

`guile-output` *file*   [Command]
    Specifies the name of the file to bind to the Scheme standard error and
    output ports.

By default both ports are redirected to syslog. The standard error port uses the 'err' priority, and the standard output port writes to the 'warning' priority.

This option has no effect if GNU Anubis is started with either --foreground or --stdio command line option.

guile-debug *yes-or-no*   [Command]
   When set to 'yes', enables Guile stack traces and debugging output.

guile-load-path-append *path*   [Command]
   Appends the given *path* to the list of Guile load paths (see Section "Build Config" in *The Guile Reference Manual*).

guile-load-program *file*   [Command]
   Reads the given Scheme program.

5 The Rule System

The rule system is a core part of GNU Anubis. It can be regarded as a program that is executed for every outgoing message.

Throughout this chapter, when showing syntax definitions, their optional parts will be enclosed in a pair of square brackets, e.g.:

```
keyword [optional-part] mandatory-part
```

When the square braces are required symbols, they will be marked as such, e.g.:

```
remove '['key']'
```

The rule system is defined in the *RULE* section. The statements within this section are executed sequentially. Each statement is either an *action* or a *conditional statement*.

5.1 Actions

An *action* is a statement defining an operation over the message. Syntactically, each action is

```
command [=] right-hand-side
```

Where *command* specifies the operation and *right-hand-side* specifies its arguments. The equal sign is optional.

5.2 Conditional Statements

A *conditional statement* defines control flow within the section. It allows to execute arbitrary actions depending on whether a certain condition is met. The conditional statement in its simplest form is:

```
if condition
  action-list-1
fi
```

If *condition* evaluates to true, then the list of statements *action-list-1* is executed.

A simple *condition* has the following syntax:

```
part [sep] [op] [pattern-match-flags] regex
```

(square brackets denoting optional parts). Its parts are:

part   Specifies which part of the input should be considered when evaluating the condition. It is either 'command', meaning the text of the SMTP command issued while sending the message, or 'header', meaning the value of an RFC822 header. Either of the two may be followed by the name of the corresponding command or header enclosed in square brackets. If this part is missing, all command or headers will be searched.

sep   Optional *concatenation separator*. See Section 5.2.1 [Concatenations], page 29, for its meaning.

op   Either '=', meaning "match", or '!=', meaning "does not match".
                 Missing *op* is equivalent to '='.

pattern-match-flags
                 Optional *pattern-match-flags* alter the pattern matching type
                 used in subsequent conditional expression. It will be described in
                 detail in the section Section 5.5 [Regular Expressions], page 31.

regex   Regular expression enclosed in double quotes.

The condition yields true if *regex* matches the *part* (if *op* is '='), or does
not match it (if *op* is '!=').

For example:
```
if header [Subject] "^ *Re:"
   ...
fi
```
The actions represented by ... will be executed only if the 'Subject:'
header of the message starts with 'Re:' optionally preceded by any amount
of whitespace.

A more elaborate form of the conditional allows you to choose among the
two different action sets depending on a given condition. The syntax is:
```
if condition
   action-list-1
else
   action-list-2
fi
```
Here, *action-list-1* is executed if the *condition* is met. Otherwise, *action-list-2* is executed.

Note, that both *action-list-1* and *action-list-2* can in turn contain condi-
tionals, so that the conditional statements may be nested. This allows for
creating very sophisticated rule sets. As an example, consider the following
statement:
```
if [List-Id] :re ".*<anubis-commit@gnu.org>"
   modify [Subject] "[Anubis Commit Notice] &"
else
   if [List-Id] :re ".*<bug-anubis@gnu.org>"
     modify [Subject] "[Anubis Bug Notice] &"
   else
     add [X-Passed] "Subject checking"
   fi
fi
```
The effect of this statement is: depending on the value of List-Id
header, prepend the Subject header with an identification string, or add
an X-Passed header if no known List-Id was found.

To simplify writing such nested conditional statements, the 'elif' keyword is provided:
```
if condition-1
   action-list-1
```

```
elif condition-2
  action-list-2
else
  action-list-3
fi
```

This statement is equivalent to:

```
if condition
  action-list-1
else
  if condition-2
    action-list-2
  else
    action-list-3
  fi
fi
```

Any number of 'elif' branches may appear in a conditional statement, the only requirement being that they appear before the 'else' statement, if it is used.

5.2.1 Concatenations

It is important to understand that conditional expressions choose the first match. To illustrate this, lets suppose you wish to store all recipient emails from the envelope in the 'X-Also-Delivered-To' header. A naive way to do so is:

```
if command [rcpt to:] = "(.*)"
  add header [X-Also-Delivered-To] "\1"
fi
```

However, this will store only the very first RCPT TO value, so you will not achieve your goal.

To help you in this case, **anubis** offers a *concatenation* operator, whose effect is to concatenate the values of all requested keys prior to matching them against the regular expression. Syntactically, the concatenation operator is a string enclosed in parentheses, placed right after the key part of a condition. This string is used as a separator when concatenating values. For example:

```
if command [rcpt to:] (",") = "(.*)"
  add header [X-Also-Delivered-To] "\1"
fi
```

This fragment will first create a string containing all RCPT TO addresses, separated by commas, and then match it against the regular expression on the right hand side. Since this expression matches any string, the '\1' will contain a comma-separated list of addresses.

5.3 Triggers

Triggers are conditional statements that use the value of the 'Subject' header to alter the control flow. Syntactically, a trigger is:

```
trigger [flags] pattern
  action-list
done
```

Here, *pattern* is the pattern against which the 'Subject' header is checked, *flags* are optional flags controlling the type of regular expression used (see Section 5.5 [Regular Expressions], page 31). For backward compatibility, the keyword **rule** may be used instead of **trigger**.

The trigger acts as follows: First, the value of the 'Subject' header is matched against the pattern '@@'*pattern*. If it matches, then the matched part is removed from the 'Subject', and the *action-list* is executed.

Basically, putting aside the possibility to use different flavors of regular expressions, a trigger is equivalent to the following statement:

```
if header[Subject] :posix "(.*)@@pattern"
  modify header [Subject] "\1"
  action-list
fi
```

Thus, adding the '@@*rule-name*' code to the 'Subject' header of your message, triggers a rule named *rule-name*, specified in a user configuration file. For example:

```
BEGIN RULE
trigger :basic "^gpg-encrypt-john"
  gpg-encrypt "john's_gpg_key"
done
END
```

Now, if you send an email with the subject ending on '@@gpg-encrypt-john' (e.g.: 'Subject: hello John!@@gpg-encrypt-john'), it will be encrypted with John's public key. The trigger will remove the '@@' and the characters following it, so John will only receive a message with 'hello John!' as a subject.

Another example shows an even more dynamic trigger, that is using a substitution and back-references:

```
---BEGIN RULE---
trigger :extended "^gpg-encrypt:(.*)"
  gpg-encrypt "\1"
  add [X-GPG-Comment] "Encrypted for \1"
done
---END---
```

To encrypt a message to user e.g. 'John', simply send an email with a subject 'hello John!@@gpg-encrypt:john's_gpg_key'. This way, you decide at a run time which public key should be used, without creating separate rules for each user.

5.4 Boolean Operators

The following table lists the boolean operators that can be used in Anubis conditional expressions in the order of increasing binding strength:

- 'OR'
- 'AND'
- 'NOT'

As an example, let's consider the following statement:

```
if header[X-Mailer] "mutt" or header[X-Mailer] "mail" \
   and not header[Content-Type] "^multipart/mixed;.*"
   action
fi
```

In this case the *action* will be executed if the X-Mailer header contains the word 'mutt'. The same *action* will also be executed if the X-Mailer header contains the word 'mail' *and* the value of the Content-Type header does not begin with the string 'multipart/mixed'.

Now, if we wished to execute the *action* for any message sent using mail or mutt whose Content-Type header does not begin with the string 'multipart/mixed', we would write the following:

```
if (header[X-Mailer] "mutt" or header[X-Mailer] "mail") \
   and not header[Content-Type] "^multipart/mixed;.*"
   action
fi
```

Notice the use of parentheses to change the binding strength of the boolean operators.

5.5 Regular Expressions

GNU Anubis supports two types of regular expressions: POSIX (both basic and extended), and Perl-style regular expressions. The former are always supported, whereas the support for the latter depends on the configuration settings at compile time. By default POSIX extended regexps are assumed.

Regular expressions often contain characters, prefixed with a backslash (e.g. '\(' in basic POSIX or '\s' in perl-style regexp). Due to escape substitution (see Table 4.1), you will have to escape the backslash character, e.g. write:

```
modify :perl body ["\\stext"] "text"
```

instead of

```
# WRONG!
modify :perl body ["\stext"] "text"
```

However, this rule does not apply to back references, i.e. "\1" is OK.

A number of modifiers is provided to change the type of regular expressions. These are described in the following table.

:regex
:re   Indicates that the following pattern should be considered a regular expression. The default type for this expression is assumed.

:perl
:perlre   The regular expression is a Perl-style one.

`:exact`

`:ex`   Disables regular expression matching, all patterns will be
             matched as exact strings.

`:scase`   Enables case-sensitive comparison.

`:icase`   Enables case-insensitive comparison.

`:basic`   Switches to the POSIX Basic regular expression matching.

`:extended`
             Switches to the POSIX Extended regular expression matching.

The special statement **regex** allows you to alter the default regular expression type. For example, the following statement

```
regex :perl :scase
```

sets the default regular expression types to Perl-style, case-sensitive. The
settings of **regex** statement regard only those patterns that appear after it
in the configuration file and have force until the next occurrence of the **regex**
statement.

A couple of examples:

```
if header[Subject] :perlre "(?<=(?<!foo)bar)baz"
  ...
fi
```

This will match any `Subject` header whose value matches an occurrence of
'baz' that is preceded by 'bar' which in turn is not preceded by 'foo'.

```
if header[Subject] :scase "^Re"
```

will match a `Subject` header whose value starts with 'Re', but will not match
it if it starts with 'RE' or 're'.

When using POSIX regular expressions, the extended syntax is enabled
by default. If you wish to use a basic regular expression, precede it with the
`:basic` flag.

For the detailed description of POSIX regular expressions, See Section
"Regular Expression Library" in *Regular Expression Library*. For information about Perl-style regular expressions, refer to the Perl documentation.

5.6 Action List

An *action list* is a list of action commands, which control processing of
messages. All action command names are case insensitive, so you can use
for instance: 'add' or 'ADD' or 'AdD', and so on.

5.6.1 Stop Action

The **stop** command stops processing of the section immediately. It can be
used in the main `RULE` section as well as in any user-defined section. For
example:

```
if not header[Content-Type] "text/plain; .*"
  stop
fi
```

5.6.2 Call Action

The `call` command invokes a user-defined section much in the same manner
as a subroutine in a programming language. The invoked section continues
to execute until its end or the `stop` statement is encountered, whichever the
first.

```
BEGIN myproc
if header[Subject] "Re: .*"
  stop
fi
trigger "pgp"
  gpg-encrypt "my_gpg_key"
done
END

BEGIN RULE
call myproc
END
```

5.6.3 Adding Headers or Text

The `add` command adds arbitrary headers or text to the message. To add a
header, use the following syntax:

add *header* '['*name*']' *string*   [Command]
add '['*name*']' *string*   [Command]
> For example:
> ```
> add header[X-Comment-1] "GNU's Not Unix!"
> add [X-Comment-2] "Support FSF!"
> ```

To add text to the body of the message, use:

add *body* `text`   [Command]
> Adds the *text* to the message body. Use of this command with 'here
> document' syntax allows to append multi-line text to the message, e.g.:
> ```
> add body <<-EOT
>       Regards,
>       Hostmaster
> EOT
> ```

5.6.4 Removing Headers

The `remove` command removes headers from the message. The syntax is:

remove [*flags*] *header* '['*string*']'   [Command]
remove [*flags*] '['*string*']'   [Command]
> The name of the header to delete is given by *string* parameter. By default
> only those headers are removed whose names match it exactly. Optional

flags allow to change this behavior. See Section 5.5 [Regular Expressions], page 31, for the detailed description of these.

An example:

```
remove ["X-Mailer"]
remove :regex ["^X-.*"]
```

The first example will remove the '`X-Mailer:`' header from an outgoing message, and the second one will remove all "X-*" headers.

5.6.5 Modifying Messages

The `modify` command alters headers or body of the message.

modify [*flags*] *header* '['*key*']' '['*new-key*']'   [Command]
modify [*flags*] '['*key*']' '['*new-key*']'   [Command]

For each header whose name matches *key*, replaces its name with *new-key*. If *key* is a regular expressions, *new-key* can contain back references. For example, the following statement selects all headers whose names start with '`X-`' and changes their names to begin with '`X-Old-`':

```
modify header :re ["X-\(.*\)"] ["X-Old-\1"]
```

modify [*flags*] *header* '['*key*']' *value*   [Command]
modify [*flags*] '['*key*']' *value*   [Command]

For each header whose name matches *key*, changes its value to *value*. For example:

```
modify [Subject] "New subject"
```

Every occurrence of unescaped '`&`' in the new value will be replaced by the old header value. To enter the '`&`' character itself, escape it with two backslash characters ('`\\`'). For example, the following statement

```
modify [Subject] "[Anubis \\& others] &"
```

prepends the `Subject` header with the string '`[Anubis & others]`'. Thus, the header line

```
Subject: Test subject
```

after having been processed by Anubis, will contain:

```
Subject: [Anubis & others] Test subject
```

modify [*flags*] *header* '['*key*']' '['*new-key*']' *value*   [Command]
modify [*flags*] '['*key*']' '['*new-key*']' *value*   [Command]

Combines the previous two cases, i.e. changes both the header name and its value, as shown in the following example:

```
modify header [X-Mailer] [X-X-Mailer] "GNU Anubis"
```

modify [*flags*] *body* '['*key*']'   [Command]

Removes all occurrences of *key* from the message body. For example, this statement will remove every occurrence of the word '`old`':

```
modify body ["old"]
```

`modify [flags] body ‘[’key‘]’ string`   [Command]
>   Replaces all occurrences of *key* with *string*. For example:

```
modify body :extended ["the old \([[:alnum:]]+\)"] "the new \1"
```

5.6.6 Modifying SMTP Commands

GNU Anubis is able to modify arguments of SMTP commands. To instruct
it to do so, define a section named ‘SMTP’. Anubis will call this section each
time it receives an SMTP command. This section can contain any statements
allowed for ‘RULE’ section, plus the following special flavor of the ‘modify’
statement:

`modify [flags] command ‘[’cmd‘]’ value`   [Command]
>   If the current SMTP command matches *cmd*, rewrite it by using *value* as
>   its argument.

For example, this is how to force using ‘my.host.org’ as the ‘EHLO’ argument:

```
BEGIN SMTP
modify command [ehlo] "my.host.org"
END
```

Additionally, the ESMTP authentication settings (see Section 4.2.4
[ESMTP Authentication Settings], page 21) can be used as actions in this
section.   To do so, you must first set `esmtp-auth-delayed` to ‘yes’ in
the ‘CONTROL’ section (see Section 4.2.4 [ESMTP Authentication Settings],
page 21). Changes in the settings take effect if they occur either before the
‘MAIL’ SMTP command, or while handling this command.

Consider, for example, the following configuration:

```
BEGIN CONTROL
  mode transparent
  bind 25
  remote-mta mail.example.com
  esmtp-auth-delayed yes
END

BEGIN SMTP
if command ["mail from:"] "<smith(\+.*)?@example.net>"
  esmtp-auth-id smith
  esmtp-password guessme
else
  esmtp-auth no
fi
END
```

It delays ESMTP authentication until the receipt of the `MAIL` command from the client.   Authentication is used only if the mail is being
sent from **smith@example.net** or any additional mailbox of that user (e.g.
smith+mbox@example.net). Otherwise, authentication is disabled.

The following points are worth mentioning:

1. As usual, you may use conditional expressions to decide what to modify and how. For example, the code below replaces the domain part of each 'MAIL FROM' command with 'gnu.org':

```
BEGIN SMTP
if command ["mail from:"] "<(.*)@(.*)>(.*)"
  modify command ["mail from:"] "<\1@gnu.org>\2"
fi
END
```

2. Each 'modify command' statement applies only if the current command matches its *cmd* argument. In particular, this means that you cannot modify already transferred SMTP commands nor the commands to be transferred. For example, the following code will not work:

```
BEGIN SMTP
# Wrong!
if command ["mail from:"] "<>(.*)"
  modify command [ehlo] "domain.net"
fi
END
```

It is because by the time 'MAIL FROM' is received, the 'EHLO' command has already been processed and sent to the server.

The final point to notice is that you may use an alternative name for that section (if you really want to). To do so, define the new name via the 'smtp-command-rule' option in the 'CONTROL' section (see Section 4.2.1 [smtp-command-rule], page 18).

5.6.7 Inserting Files

signature-file-append *yes-or-no*   [Command]
>   This action command adds at the end of a message body the '-- ' line, and includes a client's ~/.signature file.
>
>   Default is 'no'.

body-append *file-name*   [Command]
>   This action command includes at the end of the message body the contents of the given file. Unless *file-name* starts with a '/' character, it is taken relative to the current user home directory.

body-clear   [Command]
>   Removes the body of the message.

body-clear-append *file-name*   [Command]
>   Replaces the message body with the contents of the specified file. The action is equivalent to the following command sequence:

```
body-clear
body-append file-name
```

5.6.8 Mail Encryption

gpg-passphrase *passphrase*   [Command]
> Specifies your private key's pass phrase for signing messages using the GNU Privacy Guard. To protect your passwords from being compromised, use the 0600 (u=rw,g=,o=) permissions for the configuration file, otherwise GNU Anubis won't accept them.
>
> We recommend setting the 'gpg-passphrase' once in your configuration file, e.g. at the start of RULE section.
>
> GNU Anubis support for the GNU Privacy Guard is based on the *GnuPG Made Easy* library, available from http://www.gnupg.org/gpgme.html.

gpg-encrypt *gpg-keys*   [Command]
> This command enables encrypting messages with the GNU Privacy Guard (Pretty Good Privacy) public key(s). *gpg-keys* is a comma separated list of keys (with no space between commas and keys).
>
>   gpg-encrypt "John's public key"

gpg-sign *gpg-signer-key*   [Command]
gpg-sign 'yes-or-default'   [Command]
> This command signs the message with your GNU Privacy Guard private key. Specify a *passphrase* with gpg-passphrase. Value 'default' means your default private key, but you can change it if you have more than one private key.
>
> For example:
>
>   gpg-sign default
>
> or
>
>   gpg-passphrase "my office key passphrase"
>   gpg-sign office@example.key

gpg-sign-encrypt *gpg-keys*[:*gpg-signer-key*]   [Command]
gpg-se *gpg-keys*[:*gpg-signer-key*]   [Command]
> This command simultaneously signs and encrypts the message. It has the same effect as gpg command line switch -se. The argument before the colon is a comma-separated list of PGP keys to encrypt the message with. This argument is mandatory. The *gpg-signer-key* part is optional. In the absence of it, your default private key is used.
>
> For example:
>
>   gpg-sign-encrypt John@example.key
>
> or
>
>   gpg-se John@example.key:office@example.key

5.6.9 Using an External Processor

external-body-processor *program* [args]   [Command]
> Pipes the message body through *program*. The *program* must be a filter that reads the text from the standard input and prints the transformed

text on the standard output. The output from it replaces the original body of the message. *args* are any additional arguments the program may require.

The amount of data fed to the external program depends on the message. For plain messages, the entire body is passed. For multi-part messages, only the first part is passed by default. This is based on the assumption that in most multi-part messages the first part contains textual data, while the rest contains various (mostly non-textual) attachments. There is a special configuration variable `read-entire-body` that controls this behavior (see Section 4.2.1 [Basic Settings], page 18). Setting `read-entire-body yes` in `CONTROL` section of your configuration file instructs Anubis to pass the entire body of multi-part messages to your external processor.

There is a substantial difference between operating in `read-entire-body no` (the default) and `read-entire-body yes` modes. When operating in `read-entire-body no`, the first part of the message is decoded and then passed to the external program. In contrast, when `read-entire-body` is set to `yes`, the message is not decoded. Thus, your external processor must be able to cope with MIME messages.

5.6.10 Quick Example

Here is a quick example of an action list:

```
---BEGIN RULE---
if header [X-Mailer] :re ".*"
   remove [X-Mailer]
   add [X-Comment] "GNU's Not Unix!"
   gpg-sign "my password"
   signature-file-append yes
fi
---END---
```

The example above removes the 'X-Mailer:' header from the message, adds the 'X-Comment:' header, then signs the message with your private key, and finally adds a signature from the file in your home directory.

5.7 Using Guile Actions

Guile is the *GNU's Ubiquitous Intelligent Language for Extensions*. It provides a Scheme interpreter conforming to the R5RS language specification. GNU Anubis uses Guile as its extension language.

This section describes how to write GNU Anubis actions in Scheme. It assumes that the reader is sufficiently familiar with the Scheme language. For information about the language, refer to *Revised(5) Report on the Algorithmic Language Scheme*. For more information about Guile, See Section "Overview" in *The Guile Reference Manual*.

5.7.1 Defining Guile Actions

A Guile action is defined as follows:

```
(define (function-name header body . rest)
  ...)
```

Its arguments are:

header   List of message headers. Each list element is a cons

```
(name . value)
```

where *name* is the name of the header field, and *value* is its value with final CRLF stripped off. Both *name* and *value* are strings.

body   A string containing the message body.

rest   Any additional arguments passed to the function from the configuration file (see Section 5.7.2 [Invoking Guile Actions], page 40). This argument may be absent if the function is not expected to take optional arguments.

The function must return a cons whose car contains the new message headers, and cdr contains the new message body. If the car is **#t**, it means that no headers are changed. If the cdr is **#t**, it means that the body has not changed. If the cdr is **#f**, Anubis will delete the entire message body.

As the first example, let's consider a *no-operation* action, i.e. an action that does not alter the message in any way. It can be written in two ways:

```
(define (noop-1 header body)
  (cons header body))

(define (noop-2 header body)
  (cons #t #t))
```

The following example is a function that deletes the message body and adds an additional header:

```
(define (proc header body)
  (cons (append header
          (cons "X-Body-Deleted" "yes"))
        #f))
```

Let's consider a more constructive example. The following function checks if the **Subject** header starts with string 'ODP:' (a Polish equivalent to 'Re:'), and if it does, replaces it with 'Re:'. It also adds the header

```
X-Processed-By: GNU Anubis
```

Additionally, an optional argument can be used. If it is given, it will be appended to the body of the message.

```
(define (fix-subject hdr body . rest)
  "If the Subject: field starts with characters \"ODP:\", replace
them with \"Re:\".
If REST is not empty, append its car to BODY"
  (cons (append
          (map (lambda (x)
                 (if (and (string-ci=? (car x) "subject")
```

```
                        (string-ci=? (substring (cdr x) 0 4) "ODP:"))
                  (cons (car x)
                         (string-append "Re:"
                                             (substring (cdr x) 4)))
                  x))
              hdr)
        (list (cons "X-Processed-By" "GNU Anubis")))
      (if (null? rest)
          #t
          (string-append body "\n" (car rest)))))
```

5.7.2 Invoking Guile Actions

Guile actions are invoked from the `RULE` section using the `guile-process` command. Its syntax is:

function *args*   [Scheme Function]
    Arguments:

    function   The name of the Guile function to be invoked.

    args   Additional arguments. These are passed to the *function* as its third argument (*rest*).

To pass keyword arguments to the function, use the usual Scheme notation: '`#:key`'.

As an example, let's consider the invocation of the `fix-subject` function, defined in the previous subsection:

```
guile-process fix-subject <<-EOT
                          ----------
                          Kind regards,
                          Antonius Block
            EOT
```

In this example, the additional argument (a string of three lines) is passed to the function, which will add it to the message of the body.

5.7.3 Support for ROT-13

The ROT-13 transformation is a simple form of encryption where the letters A-M are transposed with the letters L-Z. It is often used in Usenet postings/mailing lists to prevent people from accidentally reading a disturbing message.

GNU Anubis supports ROT-13 via a loadable Guile function. To enable this support, add the following to your `GUILE` section:

```
guile-load-program rot-13.scm
```

Then, in your `RULE` section use:

rot-13 *keyword-arguments*   [Scheme Function]
    The command accepts the following *keyword-arguments*:

    `#:body`   Encrypt the entire body of the message

`#:subject`
> Encrypt the 'Subject' header.

For example:
```
trigger "rot-13.*body"
 guile-process rot-13 #:body
done

trigger "rot-13.*subj"
 guile-process rot-13 #:subject
done
```

5.7.4 Remailers Type-I

GNU Anubis supports remailers of type I. The support is written entirely in Scheme. To enable it, you need to specify the following in the GUILE section of your configuration file:
```
guile-load-program remailer.scm
```
To send the message via a remailer, use the following command in the RULE section:

`remailer-I keyword-arguments`   [Scheme Function]
> The *keyword-arguments* specify the various parameters for the remailer. These are:

`#:rrt string`
> This is the only required keyword argument. It sets the value for the *Request Remailing To* line. *string* should be your actual recipient's email address.

`#:post news-group`
> Adds the 'Anon-Post-To: *news-group*' line, and prepares the message for sending it to the Usenet via a remailer. Note, that this is only possible with remailers that support 'Anon-Post-To:' header.

`#:latent time`
> Adds the 'Latent-Time:' line, that causes a remailer to keep your message for specified *time* before forwarding it.

`#:random` Adds random suffix to the latent time.

`#:header string`
> Adds an extra header line to the remailed message.

Example:
```
trigger "remail:(.*)/(.*)"
 guile-process remailer-I \
        #:rrt antonius_block@helsingor.net \
        #:post \1 \
        #:latent \2 \
        #:header "X-Processed-By: GNU Anubis & Remailer-I"
    done
```

Some remailers require the message to be GPG encrypted or signed. You can do so by placing `gpg-encrypt` or `gpg-sign` statement right after the invocation of `remailer-I`, for example:

```
trigger "remail:(.*)/(.*)"
  guile-process remailer-I \
              #:rrt antonius_block@helsingor.net \
              #:post \1 \
              #:latent \2 \
              #:header "X-Processed-By: GNU Anubis & Remailer-I"
  gpg-sign mykey
done
```

See Section 5.6.8 [Mail Encryption], page 37, for more information on mail encryption in GNU Anubis.

5.7.5 Entire Message Filters

There may be cases when you need to use an external filter that processes entire message (including headers). You cannot use `external-body-processor`, since it feeds only the message body to the program. To overcome this difficulty, GNU Anubis is shipped with `entire-msg.scm` module. This module provides Scheme function `entire-msg-filter`, which is to be used in such cases.

`entire-msg-filter` *program* [args]   [Scheme Function]
  Feeds entire message to the given program. The output from the program replaces message headers and body.

  progname   Full pathname of the program to be executed.

  args   Any additional arguments it may require.

Suppose you have a program `/usr/libexec/myfilter`, that accepts entire message as its input and produces on standard output a modified version of this message. The program takes the name of a directory for temporary files as its argument. The following example illustrates how to invoke this program:

```
BEGIN GUILE
guile-load-program entire-msg.scm
END

BEGIN RULE
guile-process entire-msg-filter /usr/libexec/myfilter /tmp
END
```

Another function defined in this module is `openssl-filter`:

`openssl-filter` *program* [args]   [Scheme Function]
  This function is provided for use with `openssl` program. `Openssl` binary attempts to rewind its input and fails if the latter is a pipe, so `openssl` cannot be used with `entire-msg-filter`. Instead, you should use `openssl-filter`. Its arguments are:

program   Path to `openssl` binary.

args   Its arguments

See Chapter 9 [S/MIME], page 51, for an example of use of this function.

6 Invoking GNU Anubis

The `anubis` executable acts like a daemon, i.e. after a successful startup it disconnects itself from the controlling terminal[1] and continues its work in the background. The program reads its initial settings from the 'CONTROL' section of the site-wide configuration file (see Section 4.2 [CONTROL Section], page 18) and from the command line options.

Command line options have higher priority than configuration file settings and can be used to temporarily override them.

The following command line options are understood:

'--altrc *file*'
> Specify alternate system configuration file.

'--bind [*host:*]*port*'
'-b'
> Specify the TCP port on which GNU Anubis listens for connections. The default *host* value is 'INADDR_ANY', and default *port* number is 24 (private mail system).

'--check-config[=*level*]'
'-c[*level*]'
> Run the configuration file syntax checker. Optional *level* specifies the verbosity level. The following levels are allowed:
>
> | | |
> |---|---|
> | 0 | Display only errors. This is the default. |
> | 1 | Print the syntax tree after parsing the file. |
> | 2 | As '1', but also prints the parser traces. |
> | 3 | As '2', but also prints the lexical analyzer traces. |

'--debug'
'-D'   Debug mode.

'--foreground'
'-f'   Foreground mode.

'--help'   Print short usage summary and exit.

'--local-mta *file*'
'-l'
> Execute a local SMTP server, which works on standard input and output (inetd-type program). This option excludes the '--remote-mta' option.

'--mode *mode-name*'
'-m *mode-name*'
> Selects Anubis operation mode. Allowed values for *mode-name* are 'proxy', 'transparent' (the default), 'auth' and 'mda'. See Chapter 3 [Authentication], page 5, for the detailed discussion of Anubis operation modes.

---

[1] Unless given the `--foreground` command line option.

'--norc'   Ignore system configuration file.

'--relax-perm-check'
                Do not check a user config file permissions.

'--remote-mta *host*[:*port*]'
'-r'   Specify a remote SMTP host name or IP address, which GNU
                Anubis will connect and forward mail to. The default *port* num-
                ber is 25.

'--silent'
'-s'   Work silently.

'--show-config-options'
                Print the list of configuration options used to build GNU Anubis.

'--stdio'
'-i'   Use the SMTP protocol (OMP/Tunnel) as described in RFC 821
                on standard input and output.

'--verbose'
'-v'   Work noisily.

'--version'
                Print version number and copyright.

Examples:

```
$ anubis --remote-mta smtp-host:25
```

Run GNU Anubis on port number 24 (private mail system). Note that you
must have root privileges to use port number lower than 1024. Make the
tunnel between your localhost:24 and *smtp-host*:25.

```
$ anubis -f --remote-mta smtp-host:25
```

Same as above, but run GNU Anubis in a foreground mode.

```
$ anubis -f --local-mta /usr/sbin/sendmail -- sendmail -bs
```

Same as above, but create a tunnel between localhost:24 and a local program
(local MTA). In this example local program is **sendmail** with '-bs' command
line option. The '-bs' option forces **sendmail** to work on standard input
and output.

```
$ anubis --norc --remote-mta smtp-host:25
```

Do not read the system configuration file, make the tunnel between local-
host:24 and *smtp-host*:25.

```
$ anubis --bind localhost:1111 --remote-mta smtp-host:25
```

Create the tunnel between localhost:1111 and *smtp-host*:25.

```
$ anubis -i
```

Use the SMTP protocol (OMP/Tunnel) as described in RFC 821 on standard
input and output.

7 Quick Start

By default, GNU Anubis binds to port number 24 (private mail system), so there shouldn't be any conflict with your local MTA (Mail Transport Agent). You only have to reconfigure your MUA (Mail User Agent) to talk to GNU Anubis directly on port number 24. All MUAs are normally set up to talk directly to the MTA, so you must change their settings and specify GNU Anubis' port number as their target. This makes GNU Anubis act as an outgoing mail processor between your MUA and the MTA. Read your MUA's documentation for more information.

Then you need to choose whether you want to connect GNU Anubis to a remote or local SMTP host via TCP/IP or a local SMTP program, which works on standard input and output. In the former case, specify the following option:

```
REMOTE-MTA smtp-host:25
```

In the latter case (local SMTP program), use this:

```
LOCAL-MTA /path/to/your/mta/mta-executable -bs
```

Please note that the '`-bs`' command line option is a common way to run MTAs on standard input and output, but it is not a rule. Refer to your MTA's documentation, for instructions on how to get it working on standard input and output.

If you would like to run GNU Anubis on port number 25 (which is a default value for the SMTP) or any other port number, then use the '`bind`' keyword. For instance, the following code will bind GNU Anubis to '`localhost:25`':

```
bind localhost:25
```

This can make a conflict between GNU Anubis and your local MTA, which usually listens on port number 25. To solve this, disable the MTA and specify the '`local-mta`' keyword, or run MTA on port number different than GNU Anubis' port number (e.g. 1111). For example:

```
bind localhost:25
remote-mta localhost:1111
```

Caution: Make sure that your local machine doesn't accept any incoming mail (i.e. it is *not* a POP or IMAP server), otherwise you cannot disable your MTA or change its port number!

8 Using the TLS/SSL Encryption

The TLS (Transport Layer Security) protocol provides communications privacy over the Internet. It is described in RFC 2246 document. The protocol allows client/server applications to communicate in a way that prevents eavesdropping, tampering, or message forgery. The primary goal of the protocol is to provide privacy and data integrity between two communicating applications. The TLS protocol itself is based on the SSL 3.0 (Secure Socket Layer) protocol specification.

GNU Anubis supports the TLS/SSL (via the GnuTLS, a Transport Layer Security Library available from `http://www.gnutls.org/`), but your MTA must provide the 'STARTTLS' command first. This can be checked by:

```
$ telnet your-smtp-host 25
  ehlo your-domain-name
```

The server will response with all its available commands. If you see the word 'STARTTLS', then you can use the TLS/SSL encryption. If your MUA doesn't support the TLS/SSL encryption, but your MTA does, then you should use the 'oneway-ssl' keyword in your configuration file. Before using the TLS/SSL encryption, generate a proper private key and a certificate. GNU `anubis` provides a scrypt `keygen.sh` which can be used for this, e.g.:

```
$ cd anubis-directory
$ ./build/keygen.sh
```

This will create the `anubis.pem` file. Copy it to the directory of your choice, e.g. `/usr/share/ssl/certs/`. Next, edit your configuration file by adding:

```
ssl yes
ssl-key path-to-the-private-key
ssl-cert path-to-the-certificate
```

For example:

```
ssl-key /usr/share/ssl/certs/anubis.pem
ssl-cert /usr/share/ssl/certs/anubis.pem
```

Caution: Each client can specify its own private key and a certificate by adding the 'ssl-key' and 'ssl-cert' keywords in its own user configuration file.

See Section 4.2.5 [Encryption Settings], page 22, for details.

9 Using S/MIME Signatures

Anubis version 4.2 does not yet provide built-in support for S/MIME encryption or signing. To encrypt or sign messages using S/MIME, you will have to use external programs. Usually such programs require the whole message as their input, so simply using `external-body-processor` will not work. GNU Anubis distribution includes a special Guile program, `entire-msg.scm`, designed for use with such programs. For its detailed description, please refer to Section 5.7.5 [Entire Message Filters], page 42. This chapter addresses a special case of using it with `openssl` to sign outgoing messages.

To use `openssl` for S/MIME signing, invoke it using `openssl-filter` function defined in `entire-msg.scm`. Give it at least `-sign` and `-signer` arguments. Notice, that you should not specify any input or output files.

The following example illustrates this approach:

```
BEGIN GUILE
guile-load-program entire-msg.scm
END

BEGIN RULE
guile-process openssl-filter /usr/local/ssl/bin/openssl \
              smime -sign -signer FILE
END
```

10 Using Anubis to Process Incoming Mail

Historically Anubis was designed to process outgoing mail. Support for processing incoming mail was added in version 4.1.

To process incoming mail, Anubis must be started as *mail delivery agent* from your MTA configuration file. The invocation line must contain `--mode=mda` option, that tells Anubis to act in *mail delivery mode*. In this mode, Anubis receives the message from standard input, processes it using configuration file sections named `incoming-mail-rule` (see Section 4.2.1 [incoming-mail-rule], page 18) and finally calls local mailer to actually deliver the modified message. The local mailer must be given using `--local-mta` option.

Let's summarize the special features of mail delivery mode:

1. The mode is triggered by `--mode=mda` in the command line. It cannot be specified in configuration file.

2. Anubis uses local mailer to actually deliver messages. The invocation line of the local mailer must be given via `--local-mta` command line option. The `local-mta` settings (if any) (see Section 4.2.1 [Basic Settings], page 18) are ignored.

   The local mailer invocation line can contain meta-variables `%sender` and `%recipient`, which will be replaced by the actual sender and recipient email addresses before starting the mailer.

3. A special option `--from` may be used in Anubis command line. This option sets sender email address (see `%sender` meta variable above). It implies `--mode=mda`. If the option is not given, GNU Anubis will deduce sender address from UNIX 'From ' header or, if it is not present, from the value of `From` SMTP header.

4. In MDA mode, Anubis takes recipient email addresses from the command line.

5. Anubis uses a separate rule section for processing incoming mails. The default section name is 'INCOMING'. It may be overridden in system configuration file using `incoming-mail-rule` (see Section 4.2.1 [incoming-mail-rule], page 18).

The following discussion explains how to configure Anubis in MDA mode with different mail transport agents.

- Sendmail

  If you use `mc` file to generate `sendmail.cf`, use `LOCAL_MAILER_PATH` and `LOCAL_MAILER_ARGS` as shown in the following example:

      define('LOCAL_MAILER_PATH', '/usr/local/sbin/anubis')
      define('LOCAL_MAILER_ARGS',
            'mail --mode=mda -l '/libexec/mail.local -f %sender %recipient')

  If you prefer to directly edit `sendmail.cf`, use M macro to declare Anubis as a local mailer. For example:

```
Mlocal, P=/usr/local/sbin/anubis,
        F=lsDFMAw5:/|@qSPfhn9,
        S=EnvFromL/HdrFromL, R=EnvToL/HdrToL,
        T=DNS/RFC822/X-Unix,
        A=mail --mode=mda -l '/libexec/mail.local -f %sender %recipient' $u
```

- Exim

  With exim, you will need to declare appropriate transport and director
  in exim.conf:

  ```
  # transport
  mail_local_pipe:
    driver = pipe
    command = /usr/local/sbin/anubis --mode=mda \
              -l '/libexec/mail.local -f %sender %recipient' $local_part
    return_path_add
    delivery_date_add
    envelope_to_add

  # director
  mail_local:
    driver = localuser
    transport = mail_local_pipe
  ```

11 Using Mutt with Anubis

Newer versions of mutt (1.5.20) are able to send mail directly via SMTP channel. Older ones (1.4.1 and 1.5.3) can only use an external program to send messages.

The following sections describe the recommended ways of configuring mutt.

11.1 Configure Mutt SMTP

Mutt version 1.5.20 supports SMTP if compiled with the --enable-smtp option. You can verify if it is so by running the following command:

```
mutt -v | fgrep '+USE_SMTP'
```

If the output contains '+USE_SMTP', then mutt is compiled properly and you can use further instructions from this section.

set smtp_url = "*url*"
> Sets URL of the Anubis server. The format of *url* is
>
> > smtp://[*user*[:*pass*]@]host[:*port*]
>
> where square brackets denote optional parts. If Anubis is running in 'auth' mode, *user* and *pass* become mandatory. The latter can also be set using the following statement.

set smtp_pass = "*pass*"
> Sets SMTP password.

set smtp_authenticators="*auth-list*"
> Sets the list of the authentication methods to try when attempting to perform SMTP AUTH. The argument is a colon-delimited list of method names.

For example, if Anubis runs on the server 'anubis.domain.org', port 24, your .muttrc could contain:

```
set smtp_url = "smtp://anubis.domain.org:24"
```

11.2 Using GNU mailutils as an interface to mutt

GNU Mailutils is a collection of utilities for handling electronic mail. It includes lots of programs necessary for dealing with e-mail messages. One of them is maidag — a general-purpose mail delivery agent (see Section "maidag" in *GNU Mailutils Manual*).

The package can be downloaded from ftp://ftp.gnu.org/gnu/mailutils or any of the mirrors (See http://www.gnu.org/order/ftp.html for a complete list of these. Please, select the mirror closest too you). The complete information about the package is available from its home page at http://www.gnu.org/software/mailutils/

To use `maidag`, first download and install GNU mailutils (as usual the package is shipped with files `README` and `INSTALL` which provide the necessary guidelines). Then add to your `.muttrc` file the following line:

```
set sendmail="maidag --url smtp://hostname[:port]"
```

where *maidag* stands for the full file name of `maidag` utility, *hostname* and optional *port* specify the host name (or IP address) of the machine running `anubis` and the port it listens on. Notice, that the default port value for 'smtp' is 25, which means that in most cases you will have to specify it explicitly.

For example, suppose you run `anubis` on machine 'anubis.example.org' and that it listens on port 24. Let's also assume you have installed mailutils in the default location, so that full file name of the `maidag` utility is /usr/local/sbin/maidag. Then, your `.muttrc` will contain:

```
set sendmail="/usr/local/sbin/maidag \
                --url smtp://anubis.example.org:24"
```

(the line being split for readability).

11.3 Using msg2smtp.pl as an interface to mutt

GNU Anubis is shipped with `msg2smtp.pl` — a perl script designed as an interface between it and `mutt`. The script is kindly contributed by Michael de Beer.

The script is located in the subdirectory `contrib` of GNU Anubis distribution. Copy it to any convenient location, e.g.:

```
cp anubis-4.2/contrib/msg2smtp.pl /usr/local/libexec
```

and add the following line to your `.muttrc`:

```
set sendmail="/usr/local/libexec/msg2smtp.pl -h hostname -p port"
```

where *hostname* and *port* specify the host name (or IP address) of the machine running `anubis` and the port it listens on, respectively.

A complete description of `msg2smtp.pl` and a discussion of its command line switches can be found in file `contrib/msg2smtp.txt`.

12 Reporting Bugs

Please send any bug reports, improvements, comments, suggestions, or questions to `bug-anubis@gnu.org`.

Before reporting a bug, make sure you have actually found a real bug. Carefully reread the documentation and see if it really says you can do what you are trying to do. If it is not clear whether you should be able to do something or not, report that too; it's a bug in the documentation!

Appendix A Pixie & Dixie

- Introduction

  This document describes a new scheme for client authentication and authorization in GNU Anubis 4.x.

- Task Description

  So far the only authentication method used by Anubis was based on the AUTH protocol (RFC 1413) (`ftp://ftp.rfc-editor.org/in-notes/rfc1413.txt`), and thus required client party to use a popular daemon `identd`, which listens on TCP port 113 for authentication requests. As its primary advantage, this method allows to quickly identify whom the server had to deal with, i.e. to obtain user name or his UID. Actually, the authentication process finishes before the client sends over his first byte. Besides, this method allows to process the entire SMTP envelope. It has, however, several drawbacks, first of them being the requirement to run `identd` on the client machine, which is not always possible (e.g. on mobile devices), and may be considered harmful for the system security (due to sending user ID over the wire).

- The Proposed Solution

  Proposed are two operation modes:

  1. *Traditional* or *transparent* (also known as *Pixie* ;-)
  2. *Authentication first* (also known as *Dixie* ;-)

  A short description of each mode follows:

  - 'Pixie' mode

    - Server requires the remote party to authenticate itself using SMTP AUTH (RFC 2554) (`ftp://ftp.rfc-editor.org/in-notes/rfc2554.txt`).

    - Early processing of SMTP envelope is possible.

    - Connections between MUA and MTA are tunneled "on the fly"

  - 'Dixie' mode In this mode GNU Anubis runs its own user database, additionally translating logins (see [login translation], page 60). It also is able to keep users' configuration files (an additional option and an advantage — see [anubis database], page 60).

  Users are authenticated using ESMTP AUTH protocol. Early processing of SMTP envelope is not possible in this mode , instead it becomes possible only after the authentication is finished successfully. This mode also delays connecting to the MTA, since Anubis first has to perform ESMTP AUTH, and only after finishing authentication, does it read and process the user's configuration file and connects to the selected MTA. Of course, the client is not able to begin sending messages until he is authenticated and accepted by Anubis.

- Details

  There is a great difference between the two modes. To begin with, 'Pixie' mode provides a tunnel (or proxy), in the sense that Anubis connects user's MUA to the remote MTA without requiring any special actions from the user.

  Let's consider a simple interaction between 'Machine-A', which runs Anubis 4, and 'Machine-B', where MUA is run.

  ```
  A: 220 Machine-A (GNU Anubis vX.X [Dixie]) ESMTP time; send your identity!
  B: EHLO Machine-B
  A: 250-Machine-A Hello ID
  250-STARTTLS
  250-AUTH DIGEST-MD5 CRAM-MD5 LOGIN
  250-XDATABASE
  250 HELP
  B: STARTTLS
  A: 220 2.0.0 Ready to start TLS
  <TLS>
  B: AUTH <METHOD>
  [method-specific authentication interchange follows]
  ```

  Now, the Anubis server has authenticated the client using data from Anubis database! I'd like this database to contain, beside the user name and password, the name and password of this user on Machine-A.

  Confusing? Let's suppose that the database contains following record:

  ```
  JohnSmith encrypted-pass-1  John
  ```

  The user has authenticated himself as 'JohnSmith' with password 'encrypted-pass-1', using ESMTP AUTH, and the given credentials matched those from the Anubis database. Now, Anubis, which has been running with super-user privileges, switches to UID of the user 'John'.

  Such solution will allow for a very flexible database, that would ease the administration tasks, since users will be able to update their corresponding records (of course, if the system administrator grants them such privileges). For instance, ODBC, SQL?

  Let's return to our sample session. After successful authentication and switching to the user's privileges, Anubis parses file ~/.anubisrc. Then, based on user's configuration settings, it connects to the MTA and from then on operates as SMTP tunnel and mail processor :-). It sends the following response to 'Machine-B':

  ```
  A: 220 OK, Welcome. Continue sending your mail!
  ```

- Further details

  The above description shows that it is impossible to use both 'Pixie' and 'Dixie' simultaneously. It is the responsibility of the system administrator to decide which operation mode to use. We could probably provide for a smooth switching between the two modes, without requiring to restart the daemon... However, it is not critical. Restarting the daemon in order to switch to another operation mode is also a feasible solution.

Now, let me describe for what kind of users each mode is intended.

The traditional ('`Pixie`') mode is intended for those users who use Anubis on a single machine or within a local network that allows to use `identd`. In short, '`Pixie`' is useful when the use of `identd` is possible and safe.

In contrast, the new mode '`Dixie`' is intended for more complex setups, where a single machine running GNU Anubis serves a number of clients connecting from different machines and networks. It is supposed that no client machine is running `identd`. The only recommendation for this mode is that each user have a system account on the machine running Anubis. But then, even this is not required!

That's a feature I haven't described yet :^) As described above, Anubis database must contain second login name in order for Anubis to be able to switch to the user's privileges and parse his `~/.anubisrc` file. Now, I supposed that the database is able to keep user configuration files as well. So, each database record must contain an additional flag informing Anubis whether it should read the local file `~/.anubisrc`, or read the configuration file stored in the database. Sure enough, GNU Anubis still will have to switch to the user's privileges, for security reasons, but this can be done using usual **user-notprivileged** configuration (see Section 4.2.6 [Security Settings], page 23).

Surely you have noticed that in its response to EHLO command Dixie returned **250-XDATABASE** capability. Yes, this is exactly that command that I'd like to be used for remote management of the database records (after having successfully passed ESMTP AUTH).

Available operations are: **ADD**, **MODIFY**, **REMOVE**, meaning addition, modification and removal of a user record, and **UPLOAD**, providing a way to upload the user's configuration file `~/.anubisrc`.

This solution will free the users from the obligation to have `~/.anubisrc` on the server machine, so they, for the first time since early Anubis versions, will be able to have their *own* configuration files. Current versions([1] require that the user configuration file be stored on the server machine before the user is able to use the service. This approach requires a certain attention from the system administrator. Should the user wish to change something in his configuration file, he would have to install the modified file on '`Machine-A`' (that's how it works now, and that's how it will continue to work for '`Pixie`' mode). The new '`Dixie`' mode solves this and frees the user from necessity to contact the system

---

[1] At the time of writing this document — Anubis versions up to 3.6.2.

administrator of 'Machine-A'. The Anubis database engine is supposed
to check the correctness of the uploaded configuration file and inform
the client about the result. It also should compute MD5 hash of the file
and compare it to the one sent by the user... What for?

- A program sending user's configuration file

  Well, we're almost finished. The user will have a small program,
  config-sender, written in whatever language (C, Java, C#), whose
  main purpose is to send user's configuration file to the database. Such
  a program could even be installed on a mobile device! Notice also, that
  this program is optional, the user is not required to use it. I envision a
  situation where:

  1. A user logs in to his account on 'Machine-B'

  2. His ~/.profile invokes config-sender program. This program,
     in turn, computes MD5 sum of the local ~/.anubisrc file and sends
     it to Anubis. There it will be compared to the sum kept in the
     Anubis database, and if the two sums differ, the config-sender
     will upload the contents of ~/.anubisrc...[2]

  3. The config-sender program will, of course, connect to the Anubis
     database using ESMTP (TLS/AUTH) and XDATABASE.

  Such a program will be an additional advantage, since no existing MUA
  is, of course, able to use XDATABASE command to manage Anubis database. Notice however, that GNU Hydrant (http://savannah.gnu.
  org/projects/hydrant) will probably support XDATABASE in the future...

- The End.

  Thus, the user will simply use his MUA, no identd, no hassle :)

  Actually, the only requirement for the MUA is that it support ESMTP
  AUTH. Unfortunately, some MUA, even on UNIX-like systems, are still
  not able to use ESMTP AUTH. But in this case, the user can install
  Anubis on his machine and use it to perform authentication ;-)))

  And the last detail: what to do if the remote MTA also requires ESMTP
  AUTH? The answer is quite simple: GNU Anubis is already able to
  handle this (see Section 4.2.1 [Basic Settings], page 18).

- Summary ('Dixie' mode)

  - a little slower than 'Pixie', in the sense that the actual connection
    to the MTA is established only after successful authentication

  - does not require identd!

---

[2] The scheme implemented currently is a bit different. First, the config-sender program
issues an EXAMINE command that fetches the contents of the user configuration file from
the server. Then, it compares it with the local copy kept on the client machine. If the
copies differ, config-sender issues UPLOAD and thus updates the configuration on the
server.

  – allows the user full control over his configuration settings
  – delays processing of SMTP envelope until after successful authentication.

- PS: A couple of words about storing configuration files in the database...

  These can be stored in a special directory as usual files, then each database record will have an additional field with the name of the configuration file for the given user.

  — THE END —

Appendix B Multi-Part Message Processing

0. PREFACE

In its current state (as of Anubis version 4.2) Anubis has proven to be a useful tool for processing plain text outgoing messages. However, its use with MIME messages creates several problems despite of a flexible ruleset supported by the program.

This RFC proposes a new mode of operation that should make processing of MIME messages more convenient.

1. INTRODUCTION

In general, Anubis processes a message using a set of user-defined rules, called *user program*, consisting of *conditional statements* and *actions*. Both of them may operate on message body as well as on its headers. This mode of operation suites excellently for plain text messages, however it does have its drawbacks when processing multi-part messages.

To begin with, only the first part of multi-part messages is processed, the rest of message is usually passed to the MTA verbatim. Thus, this part can be processed by the user program only if it is in plain text: parts encoded by quoted-printable or, worse yet, base-64 encoding cannot be processed this way. The only way for the user to process non-plaintext multi-part messages is by using some extension procedures (usually external scripts).

A special configuration setting `read-entire-body` (see Section 4.2.1 [Basic Settings], page 18) is provided that forces Anubis to process the entire body of a multi-part message (among other effects it means passing entire body to the external scripts as well). However, it does not help solve the problem, since no attempt is being made to decode parts of the message, so the user is left on his own when processing such messages.

The solution proposed by this memo boils down to the following: process each part of the multi-part message as a message on its own allowing user to define different RULE sections for processing different MIME types. The following sections describe the approach in more detail.

2. MULTI-PART MESSAGE PROCESSING

When processing a multi part message, Anubis first determines its MIME type. A user is allowed to define several RULE sections[1] that are supposed to handle different MIME types. Anubis keeps a `type <-> section` association table (a *dispatcher table*) which is used to determine the entry point for processing of each particular part. If the dispatcher table does not contain an entry for the given MIME type,

---

[1] This is already possible, See Section 5.6.2 [Call Action], page 33.

the contents of the part is passed verbatim. Otherwise, Anubis decodes the part body and passes it for further processing to the RULE section. When invoking this particular section, MIME headers act as a message headers and MIME body acts as its body. After the code section finishes processing of the message part, it is encoded again[2] and then passed to the output.

3. RECURSIVE NATURE

MIME standards allow multi-part messages to be nested to arbitrary depth, therefore the described above process is inherently recursive. This brings following implications:

1. The dispatcher table must contain several built-in entries that will handle recursive descent to the messages of determined MIME type. At least messages having `multipart/*` and `message/rfc822` contents must be handled. These entries must be configurable, thus giving final user a possibility to disable some of them. Preferably there should exist a way of specifying new recursive types as well.

2. A confuguration parameter must be provided that will limit the maximum recursion depth for such messages.

4. MIME DISPATCHER TABLE

The structure of MIME dispatcher table should allow for flexible search of user program entries depending on MIME type of the part being processed. It is important also that it allows for a *default entry*, i.e. an entry that will be used for processing a part whose type is not explicitely mentioned in the table. The absence of such default entry should be taken as indication that the part must be transferred verbatim.

Thus, each entry of the dispatcher table must contain at least the following members.

type   Specifies regular expressions describing MIME type this entry handles. For the sake of clarity this memo uses shell-style regular expressions (see `glob(7)` or `fnmatch(3)`). However, Anubis implementation can use any other regular expression style it deems appropriate.

entry point

                Specifies an entry point to the code section that handles MIME parts of given type. The entry point is either `nil`, meaning default processing (thus the default entry can be represented as (`"*"` . `nil`) *at the end of the table*), or one of predefined entry points serving for recursive procession of message parts, or, finally, it is a code index of a user-defined rule section.

---

[2] Note that the code section could have modified the `Content-Type` header and, particularly, its `encoding` part, therefore it is not necessary that the resulting part is encoded using the same method as the original one

The dispatcher table can contain several entries matching a given MIME type. In this case, the **entry point** of each of them must be invoked in turn. For example, consider this dispatcher table:

```
text/plain  ⇒ plaintext
text/x-patch ⇒ patchfile
text/*      ⇒ anytext
```

When processing a part of type **text/plain** using this dispatcher table, first the section named **plaintext** is called, then its output is gathered and used as input for the section named **anytext**. Such approach allows for building flexible structured user programs.

5. CONFIGURATION ENTITIES

This memo proposes addition of following configuration entities to **CONTROL** section of Anubis configuration file. These entries may be used in both system-wide and user-specific configuration files, the order of their priority being determined as usual by the **rule-priority** statement (see Section 4.2.6 [Security Settings], page 23).

clear-dispatch-table   [Option]
This option discards from the dispatcher table all entries gathered so far.

dispatch-mime-type *section-id regexp-list*   [Option]
This option adds or modifies entries in MIME dispatcher table. *Section-id* specifies the *section identifier*, i.e. either the name of a user-defined rule section, or one of the keywords **none** and **recurse**. In the former case, Anubis must make sure the named section is actually defined in the configuration file and issue an error message otherwise.

Regexp-list is whitespace-separated list of regular expressions specifying MIME types that are to be handled by *section-id*.

The effect of this option is that for each regular expression *re* from the list *regexp-list*, the dispatcher table is searched for an entry whose **type** field is exactly the same as *re*[3]. If such an entry is found, its **entry code** field is replaced with *section-id*. Otherwise, if no matching entry was found a new one is constructed:

```
(re . section-id)
```

and appended to the end of the list.

For example:

```
dispatch-mime-type recurse "multipart/*" "message/rfc822"
dispatch-mime-type Text "text/*"
dispatch-mime-type none "*"
```

This example specifies that messages (or parts) with types matching **multipart/*** and **message/rfc822** must be recursed into, those of

---

[3] Byte-for-byte comparison

type `text/*` must be processed by user-defined section `Text` and the rest of parts must be transferred verbatim. The section `Text` must be declared somewhere in the configuration file as

```
BEGIN Text
...
END
```

Notice that the very first `dispatch-mime-type` specifies a built-in entry. This memo does not specify whether such a built-in entry must be present by default, or it should be explicitly declared as in the example above. The explicit declaration seems to have advantage of preserving backward compatibility with versions 4.0 and earlier of Anubis (see [COMPATIBILITY CONSIDERATIONS], page 69).

Notice also that when encountering the very first `dispatch-mime-type` (or `dispatch-mime-type-prepend`, see below) statement *in the user configuration file*, Anubis must remove the default entry (if any) from the existing dispatcher table. Such entry should be added back after processing user's `CONTROL` section, unless `clear-dispatch-table` has been used.

`dispatch-mime-type-prepend` *section-id*   [Option]
    regexp-list

Has the same effect as `dispatch-mime-type` except that the entries are prepended to the dispatcher table.

`recursion-depth` *number*   [Option]

This option limits the maximum recursion depth when processing multi-part messages to *number*.

6. TEXT vs BINARY MIME PARTS

This memo does not determine how exactly is Anubis supposed to discern between text and binary messages. The simplest way is by using the `Content-Type` header: if it contains `charset=` then it describes a text part. Otherwise it describes a binary part. Probably some more sophisticated methods should be implemented.

To avoid dependency on any particular charset, text parts must be decoded to UTF-8. Correspondingly, any literals used in Anubis configuration files must represent valid UTF-8 strings. However, this memo does not specify whether Anubis implementation should enforce UTF-8 strings in its configuration files.

It is possible to specify processing rules for binary MIME parts. However, Anubis does not provide any mechanism for binary processing, not is it supposed to provide any. This memo maintains that the existing `external-body-processor` and `guile-process` statements are quite sufficient for processing any binary message parts.

7. SAMPLE CONFIGURATION FILE

```
BEGIN CONTROL
  dispatch-mime-type recurse "multipart/*" "message/rfc822"
  dispatch-mime-type plaintext "text/plain"
  dispatch-mime-type image "img/*"
END CONTROL

SECTION plaintext
  modify body ["now"] "then"
END

SECTION image
  external-body-processor resize-message
END
```

This example configuration shows the idea of using **external-body-processor** statement for binary part processing. The following version of **resize-message** script uses **convert** program for reducing image size to 120x120 pixels:

```
#! /bin/sh
TMP=$HOME/tmp/$$
cat - > $TMP
convert -size 120x120 $TMP.jpg -resize 120x120 +profile '*' out-$TMP
rm $TMP
cat out-$TMP
rm out-$TMP
```

8. COMPATIBILITY CONSIDERATIONS

In the absense of any **dispatch-mime-type** statements, Anubis should behave exactly as version 4.0 did. Specifying

```
clear-dispatch-table
```

in the user configuration file should produce the same effect. This can be useful if system-wide configuration file contained some **dispatch-mime-type** statements.

9. SECURITY CONSIDERATIONS

This specification is believed to not introduce any special security considerations.

Appendix C GNU Free Documentation License

Version 1.2, November 2002

Copyright © 2000,2001,2002 Free Software Foundation, Inc.

51 Franklin Street, Fifth Floor, Boston, MA 02110-1301, USA

Everyone is permitted to copy and distribute verbatim copies
of this license document, but changing it is not allowed.

0. PREAMBLE

The purpose of this License is to make a manual, textbook, or other functional and useful document *free* in the sense of freedom: to assure everyone the effective freedom to copy and redistribute it, with or without modifying it, either commercially or noncommercially. Secondarily, this License preserves for the author and publisher a way to get credit for their work, while not being considered responsible for modifications made by others.

This License is a kind of "copyleft", which means that derivative works of the document must themselves be free in the same sense. It complements the GNU General Public License, which is a copyleft license designed for free software.

We have designed this License in order to use it for manuals for free software, because free software needs free documentation: a free program should come with manuals providing the same freedoms that the software does. But this License is not limited to software manuals; it can be used for any textual work, regardless of subject matter or whether it is published as a printed book. We recommend this License principally for works whose purpose is instruction or reference.

1. APPLICABILITY AND DEFINITIONS

This License applies to any manual or other work, in any medium, that contains a notice placed by the copyright holder saying it can be distributed under the terms of this License. Such a notice grants a world-wide, royalty-free license, unlimited in duration, to use that work under the conditions stated herein. The "Document", below, refers to any such manual or work. Any member of the public is a licensee, and is addressed as "you". You accept the license if you copy, modify or distribute the work in a way requiring permission under copyright law.

A "Modified Version" of the Document means any work containing the Document or a portion of it, either copied verbatim, or with modifications and/or translated into another language.

A "Secondary Section" is a named appendix or a front-matter section of the Document that deals exclusively with the relationship of the publishers or authors of the Document to the Document's overall subject (or to related matters) and contains nothing that could fall directly within that overall subject. (Thus, if the Document is in part a textbook of mathematics, a Secondary Section may not explain any mathematics.) The relationship could be a matter of historical connection with the subject or with related matters, or of legal, commercial, philosophical, ethical or political position regarding them.

The "Invariant Sections" are certain Secondary Sections whose titles are designated, as being those of Invariant Sections, in the notice that says that the Document is released under this License. If a section does not fit the above definition of Secondary then it is not allowed to be designated as Invariant. The Document may contain zero Invariant Sections. If the Document does not identify any Invariant Sections then there are none.

The "Cover Texts" are certain short passages of text that are listed, as Front-Cover Texts or Back-Cover Texts, in the notice that says that the Document is released under this License. A Front-Cover Text may be at most 5 words, and a Back-Cover Text may be at most 25 words.

A "Transparent" copy of the Document means a machine-readable copy, represented in a format whose specification is available to the general public, that is suitable for revising the document straightforwardly with generic text editors or (for images composed of pixels) generic paint programs or (for drawings) some widely available drawing editor, and that is suitable for input to text formatters or for automatic translation to a variety of formats suitable for input to text formatters. A copy made in an otherwise Transparent file format whose markup, or absence of markup, has been arranged to thwart or discourage subsequent modification by readers is not Transparent. An image format is not Transparent if used for any substantial amount of text. A copy that is not "Transparent" is called "Opaque".

Examples of suitable formats for Transparent copies include plain ASCII without markup, Texinfo input format, LaTeX input format, SGML or XML using a publicly available DTD, and standard-conforming simple HTML, PostScript or PDF designed for human modification. Examples of transparent image formats include PNG, XCF and JPG. Opaque formats include proprietary formats that can be read and edited only by proprietary word processors, SGML or XML for which the DTD and/or processing tools are not generally available, and the machine-generated HTML, PostScript or PDF produced by some word processors for output purposes only.

The "Title Page" means, for a printed book, the title page itself, plus such following pages as are needed to hold, legibly, the material this License requires to appear in the title page. For works in formats which do not have any title page as such, "Title Page" means the text near the most prominent appearance of the work's title, preceding the beginning of the body of the text.

A section "Entitled XYZ" means a named subunit of the Document whose title either is precisely XYZ or contains XYZ in parentheses following text that translates XYZ in another language. (Here XYZ stands for a specific section name mentioned below, such as "Acknowledgements", "Dedications", "Endorsements", or "History".) To "Preserve the Title" of such a section when you modify the Document means that it remains a section "Entitled XYZ" according to this definition.

The Document may include Warranty Disclaimers next to the notice which states that this License applies to the Document. These Warranty Disclaimers are considered to be included by reference in this License, but only as regards disclaiming warranties: any other implication that these Warranty Disclaimers may have is void and has no effect on the meaning of this License.

2. VERBATIM COPYING

You may copy and distribute the Document in any medium, either commercially or noncommercially, provided that this License, the copyright notices, and the license notice saying this License applies to the Document are reproduced in all copies, and that you add no other conditions whatsoever to those of this License. You may not use technical measures to obstruct or control the reading or further copying of the copies you make or distribute. However, you may accept compensation in exchange for copies. If you distribute a large enough number of copies you must also follow the conditions in section 3.

You may also lend copies, under the same conditions stated above, and you may publicly display copies.

3. COPYING IN QUANTITY

If you publish printed copies (or copies in media that commonly have printed covers) of the Document, numbering more than 100, and the Document's license notice requires Cover Texts, you must enclose the copies in covers that carry, clearly and legibly, all these Cover Texts: Front-Cover Texts on the front cover, and Back-Cover Texts on the back cover. Both covers must also clearly and legibly identify you as the publisher of these copies. The front cover must present the full title with all words of the title equally prominent and visible. You may add other material on the covers in addition. Copying with changes limited to the covers, as long as they preserve the title of the Document and satisfy these conditions, can be treated as verbatim copying in other respects.

If the required texts for either cover are too voluminous to fit legibly, you should put the first ones listed (as many as fit reasonably) on the actual cover, and continue the rest onto adjacent pages.

If you publish or distribute Opaque copies of the Document numbering more than 100, you must either include a machine-readable Transparent copy along with each Opaque copy, or state in or with each Opaque copy a computer-network location from which the general network-using public has access to download using public-standard network protocols a complete Transparent copy of the Document, free of added material. If you use the latter option, you must take reasonably prudent steps, when you begin distribution of Opaque copies in quantity, to ensure that this Transparent copy will remain thus accessible at the stated location until at least one year after the last time you distribute an Opaque copy (directly or through your agents or retailers) of that edition to the public.

It is requested, but not required, that you contact the authors of the Document well before redistributing any large number of copies, to give them a chance to provide you with an updated version of the Document.

4. MODIFICATIONS

You may copy and distribute a Modified Version of the Document under the conditions of sections 2 and 3 above, provided that you release the Modified Version under precisely this License, with the Modified Version filling the role of the Document, thus licensing distribution and modification of the Modified Version to whoever possesses a copy of it. In addition, you must do these things in the Modified Version:

A. Use in the Title Page (and on the covers, if any) a title distinct from that of the Document, and from those of previous versions (which should, if there were any, be listed in the History section of the Document). You may use the same title as a previous version if the original publisher of that version gives permission.

B. List on the Title Page, as authors, one or more persons or entities responsible for authorship of the modifications in the Modified Version, together with at least five of the principal authors of the Document (all of its principal authors, if it has fewer than five), unless they release you from this requirement.

C. State on the Title page the name of the publisher of the Modified Version, as the publisher.

D. Preserve all the copyright notices of the Document.

E. Add an appropriate copyright notice for your modifications adjacent to the other copyright notices.

F. Include, immediately after the copyright notices, a license notice giving the public permission to use the Modified Version under the terms of this License, in the form shown in the Addendum below.

G. Preserve in that license notice the full lists of Invariant Sections and required Cover Texts given in the Document's license notice.

H. Include an unaltered copy of this License.

I. Preserve the section Entitled "History", Preserve its Title, and add to it an item stating at least the title, year, new authors, and publisher of the Modified Version as given on the Title Page. If there is no section Entitled "History" in the Document, create one stating the title, year, authors, and publisher of the Document as given on its Title Page, then add an item describing the Modified Version as stated in the previous sentence.

J. Preserve the network location, if any, given in the Document for public access to a Transparent copy of the Document, and likewise the network locations given in the Document for previous versions it was based on. These may be placed in the "History" section. You may omit a network location for a work that was published at least four years before the Document itself, or if the original publisher of the version it refers to gives permission.

K. For any section Entitled "Acknowledgements" or "Dedications", Preserve the Title of the section, and preserve in the section all the substance and tone of each of the contributor acknowledgements and/or dedications given therein.

L. Preserve all the Invariant Sections of the Document, unaltered in their text and in their titles. Section numbers or the equivalent are not considered part of the section titles.

M. Delete any section Entitled "Endorsements". Such a section may not be included in the Modified Version.

N. Do not retitle any existing section to be Entitled "Endorsements" or to conflict in title with any Invariant Section.

O. Preserve any Warranty Disclaimers.

If the Modified Version includes new front-matter sections or appendices that qualify as Secondary Sections and contain no material copied from the Document, you may at your option designate some or all of these sections as invariant. To do this, add their titles to the list of Invariant Sections in the Modified Version's license notice. These titles must be distinct from any other section titles.

You may add a section Entitled "Endorsements", provided it contains nothing but endorsements of your Modified Version by various parties— for example, statements of peer review or that the text has been approved by an organization as the authoritative definition of a standard.

You may add a passage of up to five words as a Front-Cover Text, and a passage of up to 25 words as a Back-Cover Text, to the end of the list of Cover Texts in the Modified Version. Only one passage of Front-Cover Text and one of Back-Cover Text may be added by (or through arrangements made by) any one entity. If the Document already includes a cover text for the same cover, previously added by you or by arrangement made by the same entity you are acting on behalf of, you may not add another; but you may replace the old one, on explicit permission from the previous publisher that added the old one.

The author(s) and publisher(s) of the Document do not by this License give permission to use their names for publicity for or to assert or imply endorsement of any Modified Version.

5. COMBINING DOCUMENTS

You may combine the Document with other documents released under this License, under the terms defined in section 4 above for modified versions, provided that you include in the combination all of the Invariant Sections of all of the original documents, unmodified, and list them all as Invariant Sections of your combined work in its license notice, and that you preserve all their Warranty Disclaimers.

The combined work need only contain one copy of this License, and multiple identical Invariant Sections may be replaced with a single copy. If there are multiple Invariant Sections with the same name but different contents, make the title of each such section unique by adding at the end of it, in parentheses, the name of the original author or publisher of that section if known, or else a unique number. Make the same adjustment to the section titles in the list of Invariant Sections in the license notice of the combined work.

In the combination, you must combine any sections Entitled "History" in the various original documents, forming one section Entitled "History"; likewise combine any sections Entitled "Acknowledgements", and any sections Entitled "Dedications". You must delete all sections Entitled "Endorsements."

6. COLLECTIONS OF DOCUMENTS

You may make a collection consisting of the Document and other documents released under this License, and replace the individual copies of this License in the various documents with a single copy that is included in the collection, provided that you follow the rules of this License for verbatim copying of each of the documents in all other respects.

You may extract a single document from such a collection, and distribute it individually under this License, provided you insert a copy of this License into the extracted document, and follow this License in all other respects regarding verbatim copying of that document.

7. AGGREGATION WITH INDEPENDENT WORKS

A compilation of the Document or its derivatives with other separate and independent documents or works, in or on a volume of a storage or distribution medium, is called an "aggregate" if the copyright resulting from the compilation is not used to limit the legal rights of the compilation's users beyond what the individual works permit. When the Document is included an aggregate, this License does not apply to the other works in the aggregate which are not themselves derivative works of the Document.

If the Cover Text requirement of section 3 is applicable to these copies of the Document, then if the Document is less than one half of the entire aggregate, the Document's Cover Texts may be placed on covers that bracket the Document within the aggregate, or the electronic equivalent of covers if the Document is in electronic form. Otherwise they must appear on printed covers that bracket the whole aggregate.

8. TRANSLATION

Translation is considered a kind of modification, so you may distribute translations of the Document under the terms of section 4. Replacing Invariant Sections with translations requires special permission from their copyright holders, but you may include translations of some or all Invariant Sections in addition to the original versions of these Invariant Sections. You may include a translation of this License, and all the license notices in the Document, and any Warrany Disclaimers, provided that you also include the original English version of this License and the original versions of those notices and disclaimers. In case of a disagreement between the translation and the original version of this License or a notice or disclaimer, the original version will prevail.

If a section in the Document is Entitled "Acknowledgements", "Dedications", or "History", the requirement (section 4) to Preserve its Title (section 1) will typically require changing the actual title.

9. TERMINATION

You may not copy, modify, sublicense, or distribute the Document except as expressly provided for under this License. Any other attempt to copy, modify, sublicense or distribute the Document is void, and will automatically terminate your rights under this License. However, parties who have received copies, or rights, from you under this License will not have their licenses terminated so long as such parties remain in full compliance.

10. FUTURE REVISIONS OF THIS LICENSE

The Free Software Foundation may publish new, revised versions of the GNU Free Documentation License from time to time. Such new versions will be similar in spirit to the present version, but may differ in detail to address new problems or concerns. See `http://www.gnu.org/copyleft/`.

Each version of the License is given a distinguishing version number. If the Document specifies that a particular numbered version of this License "or any later version" applies to it, you have the option of following the terms and conditions either of that specified version or of any later version that has been published (not as a draft) by the Free Software Foundation. If the Document does not specify a version number of this License, you may choose any version ever published (not as a draft) by the Free Software Foundation.

C.1 ADDENDUM: How to use this License for your documents

To use this License in a document you have written, include a copy of the License in the document and put the following copyright and license notices just after the title page:

```
Copyright (C)  year  your name.
Permission is granted to copy, distribute and/or modify this document
under the terms of the GNU Free Documentation License, Version 1.2
or any later version published by the Free Software Foundation;
with no Invariant Sections, no Front-Cover Texts, and no Back-Cover Texts.
A copy of the license is included in the section entitled ``GNU
Free Documentation License''.
```

If you have Invariant Sections, Front-Cover Texts and Back-Cover Texts, replace the "with...Texts." line with this:

```
with the Invariant Sections being list their titles, with
the Front-Cover Texts being list, and with the Back-Cover Texts
being list.
```

If you have Invariant Sections without Cover Texts, or some other combination of the three, merge those two alternatives to suit the situation.

If your document contains nontrivial examples of program code, we recommend releasing these examples in parallel under your choice of free software license, such as the GNU General Public License, to permit their use in free software.

Concept Index

Short Contents

Table of Contents

www.ingramcontent.com/pod-product-compliance
Lightning Source LLC
LaVergne TN
LVHW060146070326
832902LV00018B/2980